YOUTHBU

100 Activities for Youth Groups

Nick Aiken

and

Patrick Angier

Collins

Marshall Pickering

First published in 1990 by Marshall Pickering

Marshall Pickering is an imprint of
Collins Religious Division,
part of the Collins Publishing Group,
8 Grafton Street, London W1X 3LA

British Library Cataloguing in Publication Data
Aiken, Nick
Youthbuilders: 100 activities for youth groups.
1. Christian religious groups. Activities
I. Title II. Angier, Patrick
259

ISBN 0 551 02003 2

Text Set in 10/12pt Times by Input Typesetting Ltd, London
Printed in Great Britain by Cox & Wyman Ltd, Reading, Berks.

Acknowledgments

I would like to express my appreciation to my colleagues in the Education Department at Diocesan House who are a pleasure to work with, and particularly to Anne Plunkett who helped to type a large part of this book. Anne is such a tremendous help and is very longsuffering.

I would also like to thank all the youth leaders in the Guildford Diocese and I hope that this book will be a useful contribution to our work among young people.

Nick Aiken

There are many people I would like to thank for helping me to write my contribution to this book, not least Nick for giving me the opportunity to put so many ideas down on paper.

A special thank you must go to the young people who have endured hair-brained schemes and 'bright' ideas, some of which worked and some of which did not – especially Ed, David, Rachel, Stephanie and Hannah. Thanks go also to my first youth group, S.N.Y.P., and to Anita, co-leader and fellow designer and reworker of ideas in the early days.

I would also like to thank the Rev. Colin Tickner, Vicar of St Stephens, and the congregation for their encouragement to me as youth worker, Belinda Beardsley who slaved over a hot word processor to produce the manuscript, and the many other people who have helped me over the years.

Patrick Angier

Contents

SECTION I
STARTING POINTS

Starting points

Are you an overworked youth leader, or are you about to become a youth leader? If so, do you ever get that 'it's Thursday night what are we going to do with the youth group tomorrow' feeling? Or even, 'help it's Friday night what are we going to do tonight? Will it be games in the graveyard again? or a repeat of that Bible study that once went well?'

If so, *Youthbuilders* will help you. In fact, planned or unplanned, spikey or cuddly, the resources and ideas within this book will help build up your youth group. All the ideas have been used by the authors with real young people, in real youth groups and real situations.

Youthbuilders is not simply the title of the book. It also describes the role of the Christian youth leader, which is to build up young people and help them to develop a personal relationship with God. Many of the pressures, both internal and external, on teenagers tell them they are worthless and belittle them, so as Christian youth leaders we need to value our young people as the unique people God created them to be and lead them to a life-changing relationship with God through Jesus.

So what helps to create a youth group where this can happen? and what ingredients help build up a good youth group?

1. Love for the individual young people in your group and concern for their needs and problems. The desire to share their joys and sorrows, to be a shoulder to cry on when life gets tough, and in all this to be genuinely yourself. If you don't like your young people, they will know it.
2. A task or aim. If you shoot an arrow without any aim, it is very unlikely you will hit the target. All youth groups need an aim, a reason for being. For some it could be to provide recreation for the young members of the church, for others it could be to evangelise all the young people in the surrounding area. For most the aim is somewhere in between, with a mix of contact, evangelism and nurture, or fun, faith and friendships. Our youth group's aim is to see young people 'in a personal relationship with God appropriate for their age, background and length of Christian commitment'.
3. Group care. As well as a love for individuals, the leaders need to look after group concerns. Is one person dominating things, is group life stale, is the room too big or too small, are the subs being collected, does the group welcome strangers or is it very inward-looking, does it see itself as a group or as a collection of individuals?

These three ingredients can be represented by three circles which have been labelled:

T = task or aim

I = individual needs

G = group care or group maintenance

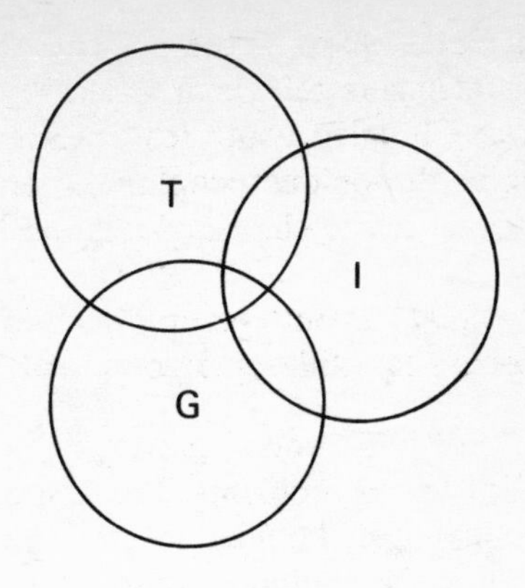

If the group is in balance all three areas will be functioning within the group, in terms of both the structure of the youth group and the programme. If the group is out of balance problems can develop. For example, too much emphasis on the task at the expense of individuals' needs can leave problems unresolved and leads to members leaving. Too much emphasis on individual needs can mean nothing is ever accomplished. So it is important that the three ingredients are kept in balance.

Youthbuilders contains a wide range of programme ideas to help do this. Each of the sections provides resources containing one or more of the ingredients for a good youth group.

Some of the programme suggestions may be very different from things you have done in the past, but give them a try, be adventurous, and feel free to adapt and change ideas to suit your youth group.

SECTION II
ICEBREAKERS

Clumping

Aim

To get the young people into groups of a particular size, and to get them warmed up and moving about.

Equipment

A loud voice.

How to play

The young people have to mingle until a number is yelled out, at which point they have to get into groups of that number and sit down in their group. Those left standing can be eliminated, or lose a chance/life, or do a forfeit. They stand again when the leader yells 'mingle'. Then the leader yells another number and the process continues.

Variations

1. Non-competitive, with no forfeits or eliminations.
2. After the number is called everyone has to touch the wall before forming a 'clump'.
3. When formed, 'clumps' have to link arms and face inwards or outwards.
4. If using lives, the two who have lost the least number of lives (the winners!) have to make the drinks, tidy the chairs, etc.

Water bomb

Aim

Icebreaker.

Equipment

Several balloons, water, an old-fashioned timer that rings and ticks loudly.

Preparation

Fill several balloons with water.

How to play

Everyone sits in a circle and the balloon is passed around the circle from person to person. When the timer rings the person holding it is out. If the balloon is burst during the game the person who burst it is out. The last remaining person is the winner.

Variations

1. Have several balloons going at once in both directions.
2. People can pass across as well as round the circle.

Zoom

Aim

Warm-up, exercise, fun.

How to play

Divide into teams of between five and ten, with the same number in each team. Each team sits in a circle of chairs closely bunched. One person is the lap counter and he starts by saying 'zoom' in the right ear of the person on his left, who does the same, and so on all the way round the circle until the person to the right of the lap counter says 'zoom' into the lap counter's right ear. You have then completed one lap.

An explanation is necessary for the game and I normally say something like this: 'We are now going to have the first ever Instep Grand Prix, and as we all know racing cars go "zoom", so what we are going to do is . . .'

Get the group to have a quick practice lap, then have several races of differing lengths, 5, 10, 2 laps.

When a team has finished they have to jump up and shout hooray and wave their arms in the air.

Variations

1. Use motor boats instead of racing cars, because motor boats go 'phut'!
2. Have a mini-competition between teams over 5 laps.

Colour clash

Aim

Icebreaker, conversation starter, discussion warm-up.

How to play

1. Get all the group to call out their favourite colour.

2. Everyone has to find a partner with a different colour.

3. Each person has three minutes to persuade their partner that they should change favourite colour to theirs, by any means.

4. After several minutes call a halt (over the row!) and find out how many have changed favourite colours.

Variations

1. Use football teams, pop groups, etc. as appropriate.
2. Have one pair persuading another pair.

Hints

A good game to lead onto something else. For example, split into teams to look at the question: 'Why are so few people persuaded by argument to become Christians, compared with the number of those who are led to Christ by friends or family?'

Magazine muddle

Aim

Icebreaker, team work, discussion starter.

Equipment

Magazines, colour supplements.

Preparation

Take enough magazines for five magazines per team, remove the staples and shuffle each team's five together, so that the pages are completely mixed.

How to play

Divide the group into teams, send each team to a separate location and give them their pile of mixed up magazines, giving them 10 minutes to reassemble them.

Variations

1. After two minutes tell all the groups (or some of the groups) that they have to complete the task in silence. Use this later as a discussion starter on communication.
2. Remove some pages from the pile so that they are incomplete. Use this as a discussion starter on spiritual gifts or group outreach.

The jelly baby game

Aim

To encourage sharing, as a discussion starter for looking at privilege, Third World needs, etc.

Equipment

Jelly babies (lots).

Preparation

Buying the equipment.

How to play

The group should all be seated and each person is given 10–20 jelly babies. Then, starting with the youngest or nearest, each person shares with the group one thing they have never done which they would like to do, e.g. visit France, have a brother/sister, live in the countryside. After each person has shared, all those people who have done the thing have to give the person sharing a jelly baby. When everyone has had a chance to share something with the group, see who has the most jelly babies and who has the least.

Variations

1. If the group is very small, then it would be worth having several rounds of sharing. If the group is very large, then it might be better to split into smaller groups.

2. There are a number of categories on which people could share, e.g.

'I wish I had a . . .' – material possessions.

'I wish I was able to . . .' – talents and abilities.

Hints

Prevent it becoming a competition:

1. By your attitude as a leader.
2. By the atmosphere of the room.

Birdie on the perch

Aim

To mix and have fun.

How to play

1. This is a great game – a real favourite. If you have a mixed group of roughly equal numbers it helps but it's not too important. Pair everyone off in as many mixed couples as possible. If a few girls have to act as boys then it will only add to the amusement.

2. Choose a suitably extrovert couple to give a demonstration of what is required. The boy goes down on one knee and the girl has to sit on his other knee. Very simple!

3. Arrange all the girls in an inner circle and all the boys in an outer circle. On the word 'go' all the girls walk in a clockwise direction and all the boys anti-clockwise. Let them go round a few times. Then, when you shout 'BIRDIE', everyone must find their partner and the girls must sit on the boys' knees. You may wish to have a couple of practice attempts.

4. When the game gets going properly, the slowest pair is eliminated each time until you eventually end up with a winning couple.

Variations

Girls have to find a partner whose knee they have not sat on previously.

Silent organisation

Aim

Mixer, icebreaker, method of dividing the group into teams.

How to play

Everyone in the group sits on a chair in a large semi-circle. Ask them to stand on their chairs.

2. Then ask them to put themselves into order of height, with the tallest at one end of the chairs and the shortest at the other. The only rules are:

   (a) They are not allowed to talk.

   (b) They are not allowed to step on the floor.

   (c) Anyone who breaks either of the above rules has to restart at the end furthest from where they are aiming to get to in the semi-circle.

3. When they are organised you can then count off into teams 1, 2, 3, 4, 1, 2, 3, 4, . . . so that there is a fair distribution of heights for a subsequent game.

Variations

Instead of using height, use age, birthdays, length of time as a Christian, or length of time as a church-goer. Talking may be necessary.

On the ball

Aim

To assist group integration and identity.

Equipment

One large soft ball.

How to play

Stand in a large circle with plenty of space between each person. The leader then says his or her own name and throws the ball to someone else, calling out that person's name. The person who catches the ball then says his or her own name and the name of the person they are going to throw the ball to. After a few minutes everyone should have caught and thrown the ball several times. By varying the pace you can keep the game going for some time. The effect is that after about five minutes everyone should know everyone else's name.

As a reminder you can play the game a few weeks later.

Hints

This ice-breaker only works with a group where not everyone knows everyone else's name. It is particularly useful when you have a group of new people joining the club.

Noughts and crosses relay

Aim

Warm-up, icebreaker.

How to play

1. Lay out a grid of nine chairs as for a noughts and crosses game with about 4–6 feet between each chair, at one end of the hall.

2. Divide the group into two teams of equal numbers. Number the teams off, 1, 2, 3, 4, 5, 6 . . . so that everyone has a number.

3. When you call out a number, the two players with that number race up the hall and sit on a seat. You keep calling numbers until a team has a row of three seats (as for noughts and crosses) or until all the seats are gone.

4. If a team gets a row they score 1 point. The first team to get 10 points is the winner.

Variations

1. Call two numbers. The first has to piggy-back the second to the seat.
2. Have all of the team except one member blindfolded.

Hint

Keep it moving fast.

The shooting gallery

Aim

To get the group warmed up, and wake up any dozers.

Equipment

Chalk, ball, coloured team bands (if you have them).

Preparation

A playing area as big as possible laid out as below.

A Team	B Team	A Team	B Team
O	X X X X X X X X X	O O O O O O O O O	X
Firing Position	Shooting Gallery		Firing Position

- - - - = chalk lines.
X=Team Members B
O=Team Members A

How to play

1. The players take their place on the court as shown above with one member of each team outside the shooting gallery.

2. The single player from Team A has the ball to start with.

(The ball can be Sorbo Sponge, football, tennis ball etc. depending on age and spread of players.)

3. Player A throws the ball at Team B. If a member of Team B is hit by the ball they are dead and join their single player outside the gallery. However, if they catch the ball they are not killed.

4. The ball passes rapidly between the courts with the numbers in the gallery reducing as they are hit in the cross fire.

5. The first team to eliminate all its opponents from the gallery is the winner.

Rules

1. If a player is hit by the ball, whichever team threw it, that player must go to his/her side's firing position.
2. If a player catches the ball cleanly he/she is not out.
3. Players in the gallery can throw at the opposition in the gallery.
4. Players can pass the ball within their team.
5. Players cannot cross the chalk lines.
6. .Balls must not be thrown at heads, but they can be thrown over the opponents' heads to your team behind them.
7. The first team to eliminate their opponents from the gallery is the winner.

Hints

The game is fast and fun, and not as complicated as it seems.

I don't believe you

Aim

To deepen relationships within the group.

Equipment

Pen and paper for everyone.

How to play

This is a game for a group who know each other fairly well. Give everyone a piece of paper and a pen. On it they should write down five true and one untrue thing about themselves.

Each person in the group then takes turns in reading out the list and the group has to guess which statement is not true.

Variations

1. You can introduce a competitive note by awarding a point each time someone identifies the untrue statement. At the end the person with the most points is the winner.
2. Increase the number of true statements. The advantage would be that the group would get to know more about each other and it could become the main activity of the evening.

Hints

1. Make sure the group understands that they should not simply put down their true statements and then add the untrue one. The aim is to slip it in among the others!

2. If you have a large and fairly talkative group this can obviously take a long time, so be ready to keep the discussion moving.

Cold feet

Aim

Icebreaker.

Equipment

For each team: 10 marbles, 1 bucket/washing-up bowl, lots of ice and some water.

Preparation

Freeze lots of icecubes and store in a freezer.

How to play

1. Volunteers come up to the front and sit on the chairs, then remove their shoes and socks.

2. A bowl/bucket is brought in for each contestant, containing 10 marbles, lots of ice and a drop of water.

3. The players have to remove the marbles using only their feet and without spilling the ice and water.

4. The first player to remove all the marbles is the winner.

Variations

Have the contestants blindfolded with a partner giving the 'fisher' instructions.

Soap shrink

Aim

Fun starter, clean-up for dirty kids, discussion starter for a session on the atonement.

Equipment

For each team: soap, a bucket or washing-up bowl, water, and more clean water for washing soap from hands afterwards. You could use one paddling pool instead of a bucket each.

Preparation

Pour water into the buckets, washing-up bowls etc. (one per team) or fill the paddling pool, and place on a plastic sheet (or play the game outside).

How to play

Divide into teams, any number per team, any number of teams. Give each team a new bar of soap (Simple is best in case of allergies).

One player from each team rushes to the paddling pool or to their team's bucket, and furiously washes his or her hands to shrink the soap.

The first team to shrink their soap into non-existence without breaking it is the winner (or the team with the smallest bar after five minutes scrubbing). The team members will need to swap over frequently.

Variations

1. Give different types of soap to different teams and share reactions and feelings from teams.
2. Have an old bath instead of a paddling pool.
3. Use a cube of ice passed round the team, instead of soap and a paddling pool.

Trust me!

Aim

To explore what it means to trust someone.

Equipment

Enough blindfolds for half the group.

How to play

1. Put everyone into pairs. One person in each pair puts on a blindfold. The partner who can see leads the one who is blindfolded all around the building for about five minutes. They can lead them by taking hold of their hand or simply by giving them verbal directions, or just by touching each other's forefinger.

2. When they come back use the exercise to discuss the feelings of those who were blindfolded – their trust in the one who was guiding them and their sense of fear and insecurity. See what theological lessons you can draw out of what is said.

Hints

You could use this activity as a lead-in to a Bible study on trust or guidance.

Ring of knowledge

Aim

Warm-up, to get them thinking as well as moving.

How to play

Everyone sits on chairs in a circle except one person who stands in the middle. The object of the game is not to be in the middle. To get a seat the player in the middle asks any one person a question. This *must* be a 'yes/no/don't know' question like 'Are you called Patrick?' rather than 'What is your name?' If the seated player answers 'yes' everyone moves one seat to the right, if 'no' everyone moves one seat to the left, if 'I don't know' everyone runs across to the opposite chair in the circle. The player in the middle tries to get a seat while everyone is moving. If he succeeds then the player left without a seat takes over in the middle.

Variations

Questions could be set on a particular theme.

Hint

Don't let the player in the middle get too near the person he is asking a question.

Follow the leader!

Aim

To have fun.

How to play

1. Choose one person out of the group to leave the room. Get everyone else to sit on the floor in a circle.

2. A leader is chosen from the group and it is the group's job to imitate exactly what the leader does. For example, they may blink their eyes, scratch their nose, shake their head etc. etc.

3. Before the action begins the person who left the room is asked to return and is placed in the centre of the circle. Just for fun ask him or her to make three full turns.

4. The one in the centre is now asked to try and figure out who is the leader. So the members of the circle need to keep a very subtle and discreet watch on their leader so they can imitate the actions exactly.

5. Once caught the leader becomes the person in the centre and is sent out of the room while a new leader is chosen. You can play this game for as long as you like.

Variation

'Killer Wink' is a variation of this game. You follow the same procedure except that you have a killer instead of a leader. When the chosen killer winks at someone in the circle, that person has to die in the most dramatic fashion possible. The homicides continue until the person in the centre has found the killer or alternatively until everyone is dead. Once caught they become, the person in the centre and leaves the room while a new killer is chosen.

Sharks

Aim

Icebreaker.

Equipment

Chalk.

How to play

Draw four circles of about one metre diameter on the floor. These represent islands. Everyone mills around the hall (in the sea) until 'Sharks' is called out – when everyone has to get onto the islands. Anyone not on an island within 10 seconds is eaten and sits out. After each round one of the islands is removed so that the players get more and more crowded, until eventually there is only one island left.

Variations

See Newspaper Couples.

Hint

Could be used as a discussion starter on co-operation and competition.

Rip off!

Aim

To have fun.

Equipment

One large sheet of newspaper for each player.

How to play

Give each person a sheet of newspaper and tell them to tear it into as long a strip as possible.

But this is where it becomes difficult. Turn off the lights! I mean, why be boring!

Make sure everyone starts at the same time and allow them four or five minutes. The person with the longest strip of paper is the winner.

Hint

When you have finished allow everyone to go and wash their ink-stained hands.

Body dice

Aim

Icebreaker. This is a hit every time.

Equipment

Materials for making two large dice.

Preparation

Make two large dice. On one, number the sides 1–6. Label the other as follows: foot, elbow, head, armpit, hand, backside.

How to play

1. Divide the group into teams of six, and number each person 1–6.

2. Both dice are rolled, and the number and part of the body called out e.g. number 2, armpit. Both dice are rolled again, e.g. number 4, elbow.

3. Now team member 2 has to connect his armpit with number 4's elbow.

4. The two dice are thrown again twice, and another connection made, e.g. number 5's hand to number 1's foot.

5. These connections are cumulative, so the groups get steadily more and more tangled. Eventually a group will not be able to make a connection – in which case they are out! The last group left tangled which is able to make a connection after the other groups have failed is the winner.

Variations

1. Change the body parts depending on age/gender of the group.
2. It is possible to have groups of seven: when the same number is called twice, e.g. number 2, head to number 2, hand, the repeat number is called as a seven.
3. If you can't make two big dice, use two coloured dice with the numbers of one colour corresponding to body parts.

Hint

Don't be too conservative! Kids will love this game and will want to play it again.

Did you know?

Aim

To deepen relationships within the group.

Equipment

Pen and paper for everyone.

How to play

This is an extremely simple activity which is usually very amusing. The time taken depends on the size of your group – it can take up to 40 minutes with a group of 20.

1. Ask them to write down six relatively unknown facts about themselves. They may need a bit of prompting so suggest things like their favourite colour, pop group, TV personality, breakfast cereal or television programme. You could also suggest things like places they have visited, people they have met or unusual things they have done. Allow about 10 minutes. Some may need to be encouraged to think hard but make sure they put down six facts. Ask them not to put their names on the papers.

2. Now ask them to fold up their paper into a fairly small piece. Collect each piece of paper in a container.

3. This is where the fun begins. Ask someone to select one of the pieces of paper and to read out slowly the six facts written down. As they are reading out the list, ask the group to guess who the facts apply to. When the person has been found, ask him or her to pick the next piece of paper.

Hints

This activity does not work so well with a very young teenage group, so you could ask them to think of four facts instead of six. Take care that the activity does not consume too much of your time in the evening's programme. Sometimes it can go on a lot longer than you expect.

M & M Olympics

Aim

Icebreaker.

Equipment

Chalk, M & Ms (sweets), paper.

How to play

Divide the group into teams. Build up scores for each team from the three 'events'.

1. **Targets**
Draw a series of five concentric circles on the floor like an archery target, labelled 10, 7, 4, 2, 1. Stand the teams at equal distances from the target, and allocate each team a colour. Each player rolls his or her M & M towards the target. Score each team's total from the resting place of the M & Ms.

2. **Vacuum**
Each team allocates two representatives, who get into position as for a wheel-barrow race. Equal numbers of each colour of M & Ms are spread on the floor. The first team to eat all their colour are the winners.

3. **Minefield**
A blindfolded team member has to walk across a designated area without treading on any M & Ms, guided by shouted instructions from the team.

Road map

Aim

To deepen relationships within the group.

Equipment

Pen and a large piece of paper for each person.

How to play

1. Give each person a large piece of paper and a pen. Tell them to draw a very small square in the bottom right hand corner, then a similar square in the top left hand corner. The first square at the bottom of the page represents the day they were born and the square at the top is today.

2. Now get them to draw a map of their life beginning at birth, asking them to represent pictorially any significant event along the way, e.g. a stay in hospital, their first school, places they have visited or lived in. Allow plenty of time and encourage them to be reasonably artistic, even those who claim they cannot draw.

3. When everyone has finished put them in pairs with people they do not know very well, and then ask them to explain to each other what they have drawn. This can be a very valuable activity, and often people discover some significant things about other people. It is a very non-threatening way of getting people to open up and begin to relate to each other in a deeper way.

Variations

After people have accomplished the activity in pairs, you can either ask them to change partners or divide them up into groups of four.

Hints

This activity tends to work better with older teenagers, although with a reasonable amount of encouragement it can work well with the younger ones.

Newspaper couples

Aim

Icebreaker.

Equipment

Old newspapers.

How to play

1. Ask each person to find a partner of the opposite sex. Give each couple a newspaper.

2. Ask them to stand on the newspaper without touching the floor.

3. Now ask them to rip their newspaper in half, and again stand on it without touching the floor.

4. The ripping and standing on the newspaper continue until couples cannot stand on their remaining newspaper without touching the floor and are eliminated. The last couple remaining are the winners.

Hints

Make sure the newspapers are torn in half properly. (The newspapers could be folded instead of being torn.)

Dominoes

Aim

To have fun.

How to play

This icebreaker is immensely simple and only takes a few minutes to play.

Ask everyone to stand behind each other in a perfectly straight line. Then ask them to guess the world record for the largest number of dominoes to be toppled. (The answer is 1,380,650 as at 2.1.88.)

You then reassure them that instead of toppling, each person has to go down in the squat position as soon as the person immediately in front touches the floor. When you shout go, the first person goes down and the sequence continues until the last person adopts the squat position. Then you reverse the process until everyone is standing up!

Do this a number of times until you have a smooth sequence and it goes very fast.

I think

Aim

To develop relationships in the group.

Equipment

Pen and a large piece of paper for each person.

How to play

Ask everyone to draw a line which divides the paper in half and then into quarters, so that they have four roughly equal squares or rectangles. Then ask them to draw in each quarter something that has been important to them or that they have been thinking about over the past month. When they have finished their drawings, divide them up into pairs to explain to each other what their pictures convey.

Variations

1. Divide into groups of four instead of two.
2. Get each person in turn to explain his or her pictures to the group.

Hints

You can use the pictures as an opportunity to have a time of prayer and to pray about some of the concerns people have raised. You will need to handle this sensitively. Also you could use the pictures as an offering to God in a time of worship; for example they could be brought up and placed on the altar during communion.

Beat the stick

Aim

Icebreaker.

Equipment

Newspaper and sellotape.

Preparation

Make a number of rolled up newspaper sticks by rolling up single sheets and securing with sellotape.

How to play

1. Ask everyone to sit on chairs in a circle except one person, Player A, who is seated on a chair in the middle of the circle. The chairs need to be well spaced. The rolled up newspaper is given to Player A, who wanders round the circle until he finds a victim, Player B.

2. Player A hits Player B across the knee with the newspaper. Player A then races back to the chair in the middle and places the newspaper on it. (It must be placed and NOT thrown.)

3. When hit Player B runs for the chair in the middle, grabs the newspaper stick and tries to hit Player A before he or she can sit down on Player B's seat.

4. If Player A gets back before being hit by Player B, then Player B is the one in the middle; if Player A gets hit by Player B before reaching the seat, Player A stays in the middle.

5. The game carries on in the same way.

Variations

1. Have more than one chair in the middle and more than one newspaper ‘stick’.
2. Players have to say the name of the person before they hit them.

Hint

Don’t allow any ‘hit backs’, i.e. the person in the middle can’t hit the person who hit him or her.

Back to back

Aim

Fun.

How to play

This game is immensely simple and only takes a matter of minutes. Gather people together in pairs. It helps if they are roughly equal in height. Get them to stand back to back. They must then lean against each other and sit down without using their hands! Very simple.

Now they have to stand up again, leaning against each other and not using their arms. Some pairs will achieve this very easily, some will not be so fortunate. But ask them to do it three or four times.

Variations

Ask them to join up with another pair and to stand in a square back to back leaning against each other. Then ask them to sit down and stand up. This variation usually produces a lot of laughs and bodies all over the floor! Ask them to do it a few times.

Hints

If they are having real problems, particularly in a group of four, allow them to link their arms together. It actually makes things a lot easier. Take care to exclude sensitively anyone who has a back problem.

M & M game

Aim

Icebreaker.

Equipment

M & Ms, straws, dishes.

How to play

1. Divide the group into equal sized teams. Give each player a straw.

2. Empty a packet of M & Ms into a dish on a table at the end of the hall.

3. The teams all line up at the end of the hall, one behind another.

4. The first person in each team runs to the dish, sucks up an M & M with the straw and runs back to the team.

5. The M & M is passed from straw to straw down the team by suction until it reaches the player at the back, who eats it off the straw.

6. The person who has eaten the M & M then runs to the dish and sucks up an M & M to pass back down the team in the same way.

7. The first team to have all eaten an M & M and to yell out 'M & Ms' is the winner.

Hint

Use wide straws, old fashioned 'school milk straws', rather than narrow ones.

Snowball showdown

Aim

Fun.

Equipment

A large quantity of old newspapers.

How to play

Divide the group into two teams. Give each team a pile of old newspapers. The two teams are then arranged in a straight line facing each other about seven feet apart.

On the word 'go' all the team members make as many paper snowballs as they can and throw them at the opposition. The winning team is the group who have the most paper snowballs on the opposite side.

Hint

This game is best with a time limit of about five minutes. It often dissolves into chaos but is great fun. They may need to wash their hands after the event as hands get very dirty.

Musical icebreakers

Aim

Icebreaker.

Equipment

Paper plates, spray custard pie mix or spray cream.

Preparation

Spray custard pie mix/cream onto several plates.

How to play

Have all the players seated in a circle as for 'Pass-the-parcel', but instead of a parcel they pass one of the custard pies. When the music stops the person who has the pie puts it in the face of the person who passed it to him and that person is eliminated. The game then continues with a fresh pie. The winner is the one who remains clean at the end.

Hints

This game is great for up-front presentations, like 'The Price is Right', or for use on weekends away.

People pyramid

Aim

Fun.

How to play

This icebreaker is very simple and can be quite amusing. You need five volunteers – or you may prefer to select five people. Tell the five that they must end up collectively touching the floor with only two hands and two feet. They must all be interlocked together but no other parts of their bodies must touch the floor. See how long they take to work out how it can be achieved. If you have a large group you could have teams of five competing.

When they have worked out how to do it, get them to hold their position for 10 seconds.

Variation

Instead of having only two hands and two feet touching the floor, a simpler version is just to have four feet on the floor.

Hints

It would be best not to use any girls who are wearing a dress or skirt as it could be embarrassing. Get those doing a hand-stand to take off their shoes.

Parachute games

Aim

Icebreakers, co-operative.

Equipment

Beg, borrow or hire a parachute. (Try local Play Resources Centres, Youth Offices, Association of Youth Clubs, any big youth clubs, community colleges, etc.)

How to play

1. **Billow Tent**
Everyone stands round the parachute, holding the edge.

Everyone in unison bends down so they are holding the parachute with the edge just off the floor.

Everyone lifts the parachute right up above their heads and takes a tiny step inwards. Stay still as the parachute billows up. (This is one of the basic moves that is used in the other games.)

Everyone steps under the parachute and pulls it down behind them to form a light, colourful enclosed tent.

2. **Cross Over**
Practise billowing the parachute. When the parachute is on the way up call a description, e.g. everyone with blue eyes, everyone who had a bath today.

When the parachute is up the people with that description run across to the opposite side.

As the people run, those holding the parachute bring the edges down as fast as possible, trying to trap them underneath.

No winners or losers, just fun.

3. **Cat and Mouse**

Everyone sits round the parachute lifting the edge up and down (not all together), so that the parachute looks like a wavy sea with air underneath.

Two people are chosen. One is the mouse and he goes underneath the parachute. The other is the cat and he goes on top of the parachute (with shoes off).

While everyone moves the edges up and down the cat has to catch the mouse. The mouse has to try to avoid being caught.

When the mouse is caught a new cat and mouse are chosen and take over.

4. **Crocodiles**

Everyone sits round the parachute with their legs straight out underneath and shakes the parachute as above.

One person is a crocodile and goes underneath the parachute.

As the paracute shakes, the crocodile grabs a pair of unsuspecting feet and drags the person under the parachute, where this person also becomes a crocodile.

Eventually everyone is under the parachute and it's time to start again.

Body massage

Aim

To have fun and create a relaxed atmosphere.

How to play

Get everyone to stand in one large circle. Now ask them to turn and face in a clockwise direction. (The fact that some will always turn and face the wrong way will raise a few laughs.) When everyone is facing the right direction ask them to place their hands on the shoulders of the person in front of them. Then massage (gently!) the person's shoulders. When they have done that for a minute or two ask everyone to face anti-clockwise and massage the person in front of them for a couple of minutes.

Variations

When this activity is finished, ask everyone to place their hands on the waist of the person in front of them and test their tickle factor. This can be great fun.

Grab

Aim

Warm-up, icebreaker.

Equipment

One chair per person, a shoe or ball or bone.

Preparation

Lay the chairs out in two lines, facing each other.

How to play

1. Each person sits on a chair. Number them off starting from opposite ends of the two lines.

1 2 3 4 5 6 7 8

×

8 7 6 5 4 3 2 1

2. The ball or bone is placed in the middle at '×' and a number is called.

3. Both players with that number try to grab the ball. The one who gets it first tries to return to his or her seat without being tagged by the other.

4. If the player gets back untagged the team score a point; if tagged then the other team scores a point.

Hint

Keep it fast and encourage them to use tactics, e.g. pretending to grab it, etc.

Week ending

Aim

To assist group integration.

How to play

1. Ask all the group to pair off with someone they have not spoken to over the past week.

2. Giving each person two minutes, ask them to take turns in explaining in detail to their partner what they have done over the past week.

3. When that has been done, ask them to join up with another pair, then each person in turn explains what their partner has been up to over the past seven days.

4. When everyone has finished, continue with the main activity of the evening.

Mirrors

Aim

A gentle trust game.

How to play

1. Everyone finds a partner. (If there are an uneven number pair one person with a leader.)

2. Ask them to label themselves 'A' and 'B'.

3. Stand a pace apart, with arms out, palms almost touching, so that 'B' is the mirror of 'A'.

4. 'A' slowly moves his or her arms and body, and 'B' has to follow as accurately as possible, without ever touching.

5. Repeat, but with 'B' leading and 'A' following.

Bumpy ride

Aim

To have fun.

How to play

This is a great icebreaker and never fails to be a great laugh. It needs 13 or more people for it to work.

Ask everyone to choose a partner. Then ask them to stand beside their partner, forming a double line down the centre of the room. Now ask everyone to lie on the floor on their backs, head to head touching their partner, and shoulder to shoulder touching the person beside them.

Ask them to put their hands in the air. Lower the odd person who is left over onto the raised hands of those lying on the floor. Then pass the person along the line.

Variation

As a slightly more civilised variation you can use a mattress or an air bed for the person to lie on.

Hints

If you have a small group, get each pair when the person has passed over them to get up and race to the end of the line so that you can keep the action continuously in motion. Then when you reach the end of the hall or room bring the person back again. Make sure that everyone lies close to each other, shoulders touching, or the support will collapse. It is best to choose someone not too heavy, and ask them to remove their shoes.

Frogger

Aim

Icebreaker, fun, warm-up, keeps them riveted.

How to play

1. Divide into teams, which can be of unequal numbers. Each team is seated in a circle. The object of the game is to get five frogs into the pond by each person in turn saying their part of the sequence without making a mistake.

2. The first sentence is: 'One frog – two eyes – four legs – in the pond – ker plunk – ker plunk.' Then for each extra frog there are two more eyes, four more legs, one more in the pond and two more ker plunks. So if there were 5 in the team, it would go like this:

Round 1				*Round 2*	*Round 3*
Player	1	says	one frog	ker plunk	in the pond
,,	2	,,	two eyes	two frogs	ker plunk
,,	3	,,	four legs	four eyes	ker plunk
,,	4	,,	in the pond	eight legs	ker plunk
,,	5	,,	ker plunk	in the pond	ker plunk

If there are more than 5, just carry on round the circle.

3. The sequence continues until all the frogs are in the pond. The first team to get to five frogs (or however many decided) is the winner and they should leap up and yell 'rivet' or similar froggy sounds.

Variations

None, unless you want to play this with millipedes: one millipede, two eyes, 1,000 legs, in the pond, ker plunk – ker plunk . . .

Talk down

Aim

To get the young people to consider what a conversation is about (i.e. listening *not* just talking!).

How to play

1. Everyone is in pairs.

2. The objective is to hold a conversation, but to talk about what *you* want to talk about, not what your partner wants to talk about.

3. Sit back and let them talk.

Conclusion

You can debrief the game and get people to share how they felt when their partner would not listen. Or move from this activity into another talking icebreaker.

Hint

The level of noise will grow progressively louder and louder.

SECTION III

ART AND CRAFT IDEAS

Introduction

Teenagers love mess. Nine out of ten parents say their teenagers' bedrooms are always untidy. Programming in opportunities for teenagers to get messy is invaluable. One way of doing this is swamp walking, another is playing the dreaded pie-filling wide game,* or alternatively you could use some art and craft ideas! The young people will enjoy these as they are able to use their creative energy as well as discovering something about themselves and God, almost without realising it. If you have never used art and craft activities in a youth group, this section will give you some ideas. It contains ten programme outlines, all of which have been used with and work with teenage groups.

Art and craft equipment is expensive, but there are ways of getting hold of it more cheaply if it is for a youth group, for example:

- Buying from a Play Resources Centre. These sell to recognised play and youth groups at nearly the same price as schools pay for their equipment. There are now several hundred play resource centres nationwide, so there should be one near you. In Leicester, as well as being able to obtain art and craft materials we were able to hire badge-making machines, parachutes and a range of other equipment.
- Buy direct from the county's central purchasing organisation. How you do this varies from county to county. In Leicester we were sent a catalogue and requisition forms,

*Details of the dreaded pie-filling wide game will be included in Youthbuilders 2.

while in Surrey we have to go to the local county-run youth centre. For a once-a-year large order of supplies this can be a very cheap source (especially if art and craft supplies are also needed for your children's work).

- Ask the congregation for old paint and brushes, paper, etc. You'll probably be surprised and delighted by what is contributed and it can be a good opportunity for youth and congregation to mix.

Face painting

Warm-up

Gurnering competition. Choose four judges from among the youth group and have the rest line up and pull the funniest, ugliest, silliest faces they can. The judges then compare notes and the winning person is Gurner of the Year and can face-paint the leader as a prize.

Equipment

Tissues, make-up remover, face paints.

Preparation

If you want to make your own face paint there are several possible recipes. Here is one:

Ingredients
Cornflour
Water
Pure soap flakes
Poster paint for washable colouring

Activity

1. Everyone who has brought face paints adds them to the central pile along with any home-made face paints. (Making them is a fun activity in itself.)

2. Make each other up in paint (making sure no one is left out, even if this means a leader joining in). Themes could be clowns, hearts, butterflies, spider's webs, etc.

3. When everyone is made up, take photographs of the group and of individuals and sub-groups. Get them developed and put them on a big card for display next week.

Going further

Talk-to:
'God loves you as you are. You are beautiful and valuable to him. You don't have to pretend to be something different. He loves you so much that he sent his son Jesus to die on the Cross, so that you could have a relationship with him.'

Collages of God

Warm-up

Magazine Muddle (from Section II).

Equipment

Magazines, PVA glue, large sheets of sugar-paper, bits of crêpe paper, tissue, newspapers, etc. (but no scissors).

Preparation

Unstaple magazines.

Activity

1. *Talk-to*:
'When we talk about God we all have different ideas of what he is like. (Give appropriate examples for your group, e.g. some may see him as a policeman, judge, clown, father . . .) We are going to try and put down on paper something of how we see God. Using the magazines and other bits we are each going to assemble a collage of God.'

2. Give them plenty of time to complete this.

3. When everyone is finished gather the group together and ask them, one at a time, to explain their collage before sticking it up on the wall.

4. When everyone has shared about their picture, move into:

Talk-to:
'We all have different ideas of what God is like, but what matters is the truth about his nature. Philip, one of Jesus' disciples, asked Jesus what God was like (read John 14:8–11). If we want to know what God is like then we need to look at Jesus.'

Going further

1. A Bible study on Jesus, his life, teaching, ministry, etc.; or
2. Prayer that the Holy Spirit will guide all of you into all truth as you look at Jesus' life over the coming weeks.

Emotions on paper

Warm-up

Some good icebreakers that produce different emotions, e.g.

Hug Tag	(from Section II)
Water Bomb	(from Section II)
Cold Feet	(from Section II)

Equipment

Large sheets of coloured sugar-paper, paints, brushes, water.

Preparation

Lay out tables, paints, paper, etc.

Activity

1. Brainstorm a list of emotions onto a flipchart or overhead projector.

2. Ask the group to choose an emotion that represents how they feel.

3. Everyone chooses a large piece of paper of appropriate colour and paints a picture that represents the emotion or mix of emotions he or she can identify with.

4. Give them plenty of time to plan and produce their pictures. When they've finished lay the pictures out on the floor.

5. Assemble the group and ask people to explain their picture.

6. *Talk-to*

'Some people say it is bad to show emotion, but God created us with emotions and all that God created is good. Hiding or burying our emotions is harmful. Jesus had emotions like us.'

Either get the group to look up the Bible passages below to discover the emotions felt by Jesus; *or* run through the passages pointing out the emotions.

Bible Passages

1.	Matthew 21:12–13	Righteous anger
2.	Matthew 20:34	Compassion
3.	Luke 13:34	Sorrow
4.	Mark 14:33	Distressed
5.	Mark 10:21	Love
6.	John 4:6	Tiredness
7.	John 11:35	Wept
8.	John 13:21	Troubled in spirit

Talk-to:

'Because Jesus knows what it is like to feel betrayed, tired, lonely, etc., he can understand our prayers when we turn to him, and it is when we are open to his Spirit that he can heal our emotional scars.'

Animals that are me

Warm-up

Barnyard
King of the Jungle
Bunnies

Equipment

Clay, plastic sheeting.

Preparation

Cover tables with plastic sheeting if they will be ruined by the clay. Divide clay into good-sized chunks (one per person).

Activity

1. Give everyone a chunk of clay, and ask them to work it so it goes soft and malleable.

2. When the clay is good and soft they are to use it to make an animal that is like themselves. It can be a real animal, present or extinct, e.g. a tiger or a tyrannosaurus; or it could be an imaginary or fictional animal.

3. When they have all finished their animal (this may or may not include painting, etc.) gather the group together. If the group is very large you may need to divide into sub-groups. Ask them in turn to show their animal to the group and talk about how it is like them (leaders should take part in this too).

4. After everyone has shared, have a feedback time, either

verbally or in writing, when people can make comments or ask questions about other people's animals.

5. Finish with animal biscuits and drinks.

Going further

This is a great introduction for a short talk on a number of different subjects, such as:

1. We are made in the image of God – the characteristics that separate men from animals, what the Bible says, and how we live out the reality of being in the image of God in practice.

2. Everyone is different, we all have different gifts, both natural and spiritual, different does not mean better or worse, all gifts are needed for the Church to fulfil Christ's commission.

Badge making

Warm-up

Who am I? (from Section II).

Equipment

Badge-making machine, disc cutter and badge parts, paper, pens, crayons, coloured foils, glue, stencils, etc.

Preparation

Hire or borrow a badge-making machine (from large youth clubs, play resource centres, community colleges, diocesan youth office, youth club association, etc.). Buy sufficient badge parts for everyone to have several badges each.

Activity

1. Demonstrate how the machine works so everyone can make their own badges.

2. Let everyone design and make a badge of their own choice. This will let them get used to the machine and see how the paper disc is larger than the visible part of the badge.

3. Then ask them to make a specific badge, e.g.

   (a) a badge that is like them, or
   (b) a badge that reflects where they are spiritually, or
   (c) a badge with a Christian message, or
   (d) a group badge.

4. When they have all made their badges gather everyone together.

Going further

1. You could show the Scripture Union video *The Stranger* and use the discussion material included with it.

or

2. Ask everyone to explain their badge and why they have made it like it is.

and/or

3. Divide into groups and answer the following questions:

   (a) What badges do people wear in your experience?
   (b) Do badges mean people are the genuine article? Why? Can you think of examples from your own experience?
   (c) What badges do Christians wear?

Bring the groups back together and have a feedback session.

Conclusion

Then conclude. There is only one badge of the Christian: 'You were marked in him with a seal, the promised Holy Spirit' (Ephesians 1:13). The sign that someone is a Christian is the presence of the Holy Spirit within.

Graffiti boards

Equipment

A1 paper or bigger (e.g. wallpaper backing paper) and backing boards (e.g. 8 ft × 4 ft hardboard or chipboard). Paste the paper, or attach it firmly, to the backing board. Mount the board, with long side horizontal, about 2 ft off the ground.

Activity

Choose your topic and ask the young people to express their views on the board. They can use words, cartoons, poems, raps – anything.

Going further

Use the reactions and views expressed as a basis for discussion groups, or for Bible study.

Hints

The bigger the board the better, because then spray paint and thick marker pens can be used.

Topics could include:

School	Boys	My town
Work	Girls	God
Parents	War	Church
Loneliness	Love	

Cardboard construction

Equipment

Staple guns
Hacksaw
Nuts, bolts
Spanner
Stanley knives
Scissors
Paint
Drill (hand or electric)

Many of these tools are dangerous if not used properly, but with supervision and teaching, young people are perfectly able to use them.

Preparation

Collect as much cardboard as you can over the preceding month, especially large sheets. Get the inner tubes of paper and fabric rolls (up to 4m long), as these make the structural frame to build on.

Activity

Using the materials build a construction of your choice, for example:

for a church service: Noah's ark, the ark of the covenant, Jericho, Herod's palace, the Easter tomb, etc.

just for fun: pirate ship, space station, rocket, sports car, tank, etc.

Anything is possible! Follow these basic principles:

1. Choose what you want to build.
2. Draw a plan from all angles.

3. Produce a frame.
4. Put cardboard sheeting onto frame.
5. Paint final details.

Hints

We had great fun building a space ship and ended up surprised by how much it weighed and how solid it was. All the materials were obtained free from local firms and from the City Council recycling centre. The young people loved it.

Body modelling

Warm-up

Some good active games to get everyone warm.

Equipment

Vaseline, Mod-roc, paint.

Activity

1. Divide into pairs.

2. Each pair is to make a plaster cast of a part of each other's body, e.g. hand, foot, arm, nose, etc. This is done by smearing the chosen part with Vaseline, then wrapping it in wetted strips of Mod-roc. When there is a good thickness, the bandaging is left to dry. When set sufficiently to hold its shape, either slide it off, or carefully cut it free and plaster the cut over.

3. When all the plaster casts are dry,

(a) paint them and/or
(b) assemble them, or
(c) mount them (like trophies).

4. *Talk-to*:
There are a number of different aspects you could talk on after this activity:

(a) There are many different gifts that make up the body of Christ; we all have at least one gift (everyone has made something, it might only be a finger). Together we have many gifts (different parts of body), etc.

(b) The casting doesn't have any life. It may be modelled on the arm and be the image of an arm but, unless it has the arm itself inside it, it cannot move. In the same way we may be made in the image of God, but without the Spirit within us we are as spiritually dead and lifeless as the plaster.

Masks

Warm-up

Some icebreakers.

Equipment

Paper bags, string, paint, paper, newspaper, glue, cardboard boxes, chicken wire, scissors, balloons.

Preparation

Collect all the equipment.

Activity

Everyone makes themselves a mask for a situation of their choice, e.g. home, school, with friends.

Paper bag masks Large paper bags, or paper carrier bags. Stick bits on, paint, cut out holes, etc. as appropriate.

Balloon masks Blow up a balloon, tie a knot, then coat one half in layers of papier-mâché (newspaper soaked in wall-paper paste). Then build up nose, chin, mouth shapes, etc. When dry cut out eyes and mouth, paint, stick on string hair, etc.

Papier-mâché wire masks Using the chicken wire as a frame, build up the layers of papier-mâché. Allow to dry, then paint, etc. as for balloon masks. These masks are stronger.

Cardboard box masks One or more cardboard boxes can be

cut up and stuck together using tape and glue. Then paint and decorate the boxes. These are good for animal masks, as it is easier to add ears and noses, etc.

When everyone has made their mask, or while they are drying, divide into groups and give them the questionnaire. When they have completed it get feedback from all the groups.

Questionnaire

1. What masks do your friends wear?
2. What masks do you wear:
   a) at school?
   b) at church?
   c) at home?
   d) with friends?
3. What stops you being yourself in these different situations?
4. How does God see you?

Talk-to:

1. God sees you as you are. You can hide (like Adam in the garden), or run away, but God knows you.

2. God loves you as you are and accepts you as you are. You don't have to be someone different for God to love you.

3. God wants you to be real and to get rid of your masks and begin a new life with him.

Close with prayer.

Hints

Papier-mâché can take a long time to dry, so you may have to do this activity over two weeks, or replace papier-mâché with Mod-roc, which dries more quickly.

Armour of God

Warm-up

Beat the Stick (from Section II).

Equipment

Newspaper, sellotape, paper, pens.

Activity

1. Read to the group Ephesians 6:10–18, and put the following list up on a flipchart:

The armour of God

Belt of Truth

Breastplate of Righteousness

Gospel Shoes?

Shield of Faith

Helmet of Salvation

Sword of the Spirit

2. Divide into pairs (if numbers are uneven put a leader with the one left over).

3. Each pair chooses a champion to be dressed in the armour of God, and a dresser.

4. Each pair is given a reel of sellotape, the newspapers are put in a pile on the floor, and the dressers are told that they have to dress their champion in the armour of God.

5. After about 20 minutes, judge the best armour.

6. Divide the group into six sub-groups. Give them each a part of the armour and ask them to write down the characteristics of their part.

7. Report back as a whole group.

8. Close with prayer.

SECTION IV

FAITHBUILDERS

St Valentine's Day

Aim

To get the young people thinking about their attitudes to relationships and the opposite sex.

Warm-ups

1. Hug Tag.
2. Get one of the leaders to give a short funny talk on his/her first date.

Preparation

1. Write out about eight poems on relationships on large sheets of paper and stick them up around the room.

2. Make Valentine cards consisting of two sheets of A4, the one on top decorated like a Valentine card, e.g. with a big red heart on it. This is sellotaped along the top edge onto the other sheet which has a dating tip or some advice written on it. Make enough cards for each member to have (at least) one. The cards are then stuck to a wall.

3. Make one large Valentine card and on the inside draw the 'slippery slope' of relationships (see below).

Main session

1. Ask everyone to read all the poems and choose the one they like the most and the one they like the least.

2. Come together and ask for any comments. Vote on the favourite and most disliked poems. Re-read the favourite.

3. Get the group to sit in a semi-circle around the part of the wall with the Valentine cards on it. Ask one person to go and choose a card and to open it and read out the tip/advice. Get the group to discuss what they think of this tip and then get the next person to open a card and so on until all the smaller cards are opened.

4. Ask for a volunteer to open the last (larger) card (they will all be dying to know what is in this special one).

5. The leader gives a short talk on the 'slippery slope' of relationships using the idea of the meanings of the colours of the traffic lights to suggest what actions should be allowed in any relationship (green), what actions should be allowed in girlfriend/boyfriend relationships (orange), and what actions should be reserved only for marriage.

6. The group may then wish to discuss where they think the zone margins should be.

Conclusion

This session does not really need any formal conclusion as the theme is discussed as it goes along, but you may wish to end by giving a very short talk on the biblical basis of marriage and what actions are reserved only for it (and why).

Hints

Keep this session humorous and encourage lively discussion.

Poems: We used Steve Turner's 'Up to Date'.

Dating tips: Have some funny/outrageous ones and some that are more serious. We used the following:

1. There is no need to go out with someone just because everyone else has a girl/boyfriend.

2. Never go further (physically) on a date than you feel happy about.

3. Holiday romances should be enjoyed while they happen but not taken too seriously.

4. Relationships over long distances or where people see each other only occasionally are unbalanced and should be avoided.

5. More fun is had in large mixed groups than in introverted couples.

6. Real relationships bear no resemblance to the romantic stories in magazines.

7. Girls should beware that boys are more easily 'turned on' than they are, so they should think more about what they wear and how they should act.

8. Boys should beware that girls form stronger emotional attachments in relationships and can be more easily hurt.

9. Both partners should accept equal financial responsibility on dates.

10. If you have a crush on someone it is always a good idea to go up to them, hug them and kiss them passionately whilst telling them you love them madly.

11. Always try to remain friends after breaking up.

12. Members of this youth group should not go out with one another.

This works best with a mixed group for obvious reasons!

The Slippery Slope:

INTENSITY

	A smile across the room	Green
	Arm around the shoulder	
T	Holding hands	
	Holding hands and squeeze	
I	The little goodnight kiss	Orange
	The big kiss	
M	Feeling outside clothes	
	Feeling inside clothes	Red
E	Heavy petting	
	Sexual intercourse	

Family favourites

Aim

To explore what the young people think about their family relationships, and to make them a more positive influence within their family.

Warm-up

Relaxation and trust games.

Equipment

Two large sheets of paper for charts and a marker pen. Lots of small cards (six per person) and pens.

Preparation

Produce enough copies of the questionnaire for each member to have one.

Main session

1. Give three small cards to each person and ask them to write on each card one of the things which cause divisions within their family.

2. Write each cause of division on a chart and vote on the top three.

3. Divide into groups and act out the three situations.

4. Give each person a questionnaire. Ask them to fill it in and then discuss it in groups.

5. Give three more cards to each person and repeat, this time writing the three things which often produce harmony and bring the family together.

6. Vote for the top three as in (2).

7. Go back into groups and re-enact the three divisive situations from before, but this time try to bring harmony into the situation.

Conclusion

Group feedback on what they felt about the session. Leader sums up and explains God's hope for the family.

Family favourites questionnaire

1. What is the best thing about being in a family?
2. What is the worst thing about being in a family?
3. How many brothers and sisters do you have?

4. Does a family have to be together to be a family?

5. How much are grandparents a part of your family?

6. What is your happiest family memory?

7. What is your funniest family memory?

8. Have you ever wanted to be in another family? If so, why?

9. Who would you like to be in your family who is not in it already? Why?

My family and other animals

Aim

To look at some of the problems young people experience at home from a Christian perspective.

Warm-up

Just a Minute. Volunteers draw a card and have to talk for one minute on the subject written on it without hesitating, repeating themselves, saying 'err', 'um', etc.

Topics: My Favourite Holiday
Christmas
Brothers and Sisters
The Perfect Mother
Washing Up
Elephants and Ants
Rivers
This Week's TV
My Favourite Soap
The Worst Pop Record

Make up as many as you need with a mix of funny and serious ones.

Preparation

1. Multiple choice papers – one for each person. (See p. 100)
2. Question papers – one for each group. (See over)
3. Bible verse papers – one for each group. (See p. 100)

Main session

The title of today's session comes from a book by Gerald Durrell. Most of us feel at some time or other that families have their negatives as well as positives. (Give example of little boy who ran away from home, but didn't get far because he was not allowed to cross the road.)

1. Give out the multiple choice papers and give everyone a few minutes to answer the questions.

2. Divide into groups of 4, 5 or 6, and get each person in turn to share their answers and explain 'why'.

3. Give the sheet of questions to each group for discussion.

4. Get the groups to report back.

5. Give each group the Bible verses to read and after reading them get them to answer the following question:

'How do you plan to do better yourself as a parent?'

6. Close with prayer.

My Family and Other Animals – Questions

1. What's the difference between unselfishness and being a doormat?

2. What difference does being a Christian make to my attitude towards my parents?

3. When parents are unreasonable, can young people go on obeying them?

4. When is the right age to leave home?

5. When do your responsibilities to your parents end?

My Family and Other Animals – Bible Verses

If you want to be great in God's kingdom be the servant of all.

Honour your father and mother (love your parents).

Multiple choice paper

Tick one answer in each section.

1. Your younger brother/sister has moved to the same school as you. It is his/her first day at school. Do you:

(a) Ignore him/her completely?
(b) Arrange for your friends to play tricks on him/her all day?
(c) Show him/her round and introduce him/her to your friends?
(d) Check at lunch and break that he/she is OK but otherwise let him/her get on by him/herself?
(e) Play truant and try to change schools?

2. It is your parents' anniversary and they have arranged to go out for the evening. You want to go out with friends but have been told to babysit for little brother/sister. Do you:

(a) Tell your parents you are going out anyway and storm out in a bad temper?
(b) Ring your friends and explain that you won't be able to go out that evening?
(c) Bribe the next door neighbour's eldest daughter to come and babysit for you?
(d) Explain the situation to your parents and listen to their suggestions?
(e) Invite all your friends round for a party now your parents are out of the way?

3. You have been told by your parents that you have to be

home from a friend's party by 10.30 p.m. and that will mean leaving the party early. Do you:

(a) Tell your parents you missed the bus as you creep in at 1.00 a.m. and find them waiting up for you?
(b) Try and reason with your parents that 10.30 is too early, but if they don't change their minds be in on time?
(c) Tell them it's not worth going and storm o to your room in a sulk?
(d) Ring a friend and get one of his/her parents to try and persuade yours that 10.30 is too early?
(e) Do as your parents say without question and get in by 10.00 to be certain you're not late?

4. One of your parents is ill in bed and you are the only other person at home. Do you:

(a) Go out to avoid catching it?
(b) Stay in but ignore them unless they call for anything?
(c) Check regularly that they have everything they want and do a few household tasks that need doing?
(d) Invite a few friends round and forget about him/her?
(e) Wait for the rest of the family to get back then moan at them for leaving you with him/her?

Jilted

Aim

To compare the promises made in relationships with the promises made at confirmation. Also by looking at human relationships to think more clearly about relationship with God. (This programme relates specifically to groups in churches which have confirmation. It can be adapted for use in other church groups.)

Warm-up

Set the atmosphere with romantic music. Play some Trust Games, or do 'face-feeling'.

Main session

Part I

1. Divide into groups of 4 – 6 and use as many of the situations below as you have groups.

   A. Samantha and John have been going out for three months and getting on really well, then John goes off with Tracey at a party.
      (i) Imagine the situation and suggest how all three might be feeling.
      (ii) What was their commitment to each other?

   B. Angela and Jeremy have been friends since they were in junior school and have been engaged for three months. The wedding is only six months away when Angela decides she wants to hitch-hike around the world instead.

(i) How do you think the two people feel about Angela's decision and why she might want to do this?
(ii) What was their commitment to each other?

C. Richard and Victoria have been married for three years and their first baby is due in two months' time, when Richard has an affair with his secretary at work and leaves Victoria.
(i) Imagine how you would feel in this situation, and suggest why it might have developed that way.
(ii) What commitment should the couple have to each other?

2. In turn each group should report back to the whole group with their answers to the questions.

3. Discuss with the whole group:

(i) Why should a person be committed to another person?
(ii) When should the interest of the other person come above self-interest?

Part II

1. Divide into two groups: Confirmed and Unconfirmed.

2. Confirmed Group: Read through some of the promises on a confirmation card.
(i) How does everyone feel about the promises which they made at confirmation?
(ii) Why do we take some commitments more seriously than others?
(iii) Does God feel jilted by the way we have kept our confirmation promises?

3. Unconfirmed Group:
(i) To what extent are we prepared to be committed to God?
(ii) Has anyone considered making a statement of commitment, i.e. getting confirmed?

(iii) In the three situations above, who did you feel most sympathy for and why?
(iv) Can people ever be committed to anything or anyone other than themselves?

Conclusion

End with a challenge, e.g. outlining areas of re-commitment. Close with a prayer.

Hint

The group situations in Part I need to be dynamic, with people getting into the situations, possibly acting them out.

Bible favourites

Aim

To encourage the group to use their Bibles, to teach biblical themes and truths.

Equipment

Paper, card, paint, pencils, crayons, face paint, glue, string, sellotape, etc. (The whole contents of your art and craft box!)

Main session

1. Get the group to divide themselves into groups of between four and six. (If they are very 'cliquey' divide them up yourself, e.g. play Clumping version 2 from Section II).

2. Each group has 45 minutes to decide their favourite Bible passage and prepare a presentation on the passage or the theme of the passage. The presentation can take any form, e.g. dance, mime, drama, sculpture, painting, sermon.

3. After 45 minutes bring the groups back together and get them to present their biblical favourite in front of the others.

4. Close with refreshments.

Variation

One-prop parables:

1. Split into groups as above.
2. Give each group a 'prop' (anything).

3. They have to act out the parable using the 'prop' as many times as possible.

Air waves

Aim

To get the young people to think about what they listen to.

Warm-up

Grab (from Section II).

Equipment

Paper, pens, Pritt-sticks, lyrics to Top Ten/Twenty songs (one per group member).

Preparation

Cut up the song lyrics into their individual lines. Put the first lines aside, then mix up the rest.

Main session

1. Put the mixed-up lines onto the floor in a pile. Give each person the first line to one song.

2. Ask them to assemble their song on a blank piece of paper on the wall one line at a time, i.e. they run to the pile and find line two and stick it below line one; run back to the pile and find line three, stick it below line two, and so on until they have all finished their song.

3. Give each person a sheet of paper and a pen. Ask them to write three things they like about their song and three things they dislike.

4. Get the group back together and share the things they like and dislike about their songs.

5. Give a short talk on the positive, negative and neutral lyrics of pop music.

> *Positive*: Those which affirm Christian principles.
>
> *Negative*: Those which oppose Christian principles.
>
> *Neutral*: Those which do not fall into either of the above.

Conclusion

Discuss what our response should be to the negative type of songs.

Hints

The talk should cover:
(a) The 'Rock Gospel' debate.
(b) Back tracking.
(c) Redemptive, separative, supportive attitudes.

Filled with the Spirit

Aim

To teach the need to be filled with and to continue being filled with the Spirit.

Warm-up

True or False Questionnaire (see below).

Equipment

Buckets (two per team), sponges (or cups with holes in – one per person).

Preparation

There are enough activities for two sessions, so decide how much you are going to do. If you are doing it all in one week you will need to prepare the True or False questionnaires (two for each person), copies of the Discussion Starters (one per team), pictures of coffee pots and the jigsaw parcels.

Main session

1. If possible take the group outside. Divide them into teams of beween four and eight, with the same number in each team. Each team lines up by a bucket full of water. Place an empty bucket 10–15 metres away from each team's bucket.

2. Each team member is then given a sponge (or a plastic cup with holes in it) and the teams have to transfer as much water

as possible from the full bucket to the empty bucket – using the sponges – in three minutes.

3. After three minutes measure how much has been transferred and announce the winners. (If you have a group where people hang around outside this is a great session to draw them in, intrigued by what is going on!)

4. Return inside for a debrief and discussion:
(a) Who won? Why?
(b) What made the task dicult?
(c) What would have happened if the bucket had been further away?
(d) How did you feel: (i) About the task? (ii) About how the other teams were doing?
(e) Did anyone think any God thoughts during the game?

5. *Talk-to*: We are thinking about the Holy Spirit. In the Bible the person of the Holy Spirit is compared to a stream of living water (John 4:14–15). All of us are rather like the sponge (or the cup) because we leak and constantly need to be re-immersed or we dry out. Or, to give another example (put up the pictures of the coee pots):

(a) We are like a coee pot.
(b) The Holy Spirit is like the water in the pot.
(c) We can save the water for ourselves or pour it out.
(d) If we pour the water out we dry up unless . . .
(e) We take our tops o and allow God to refill us.

Give the opportunity for people to ask questions on anything they didn't understand.

6. Divide back up into the teams and give each team the Discussion Starters. Give the groups about 10–15 minutes (longer if necessary) for discussion. (See p. 113)

7. Draw them back together, then get the groups to share in turn the answers to question 4.

8. Sum up the replies and either close in prayer or move on into the Going Further section.

Going further

The Gifts of the Spirit

1. Give each member of the group à parcel (prepared beforehand). Some should be brightly wrapped, some in plain paper. Each parcel contains a piece or pieces of a jigsaw.

2. Everyone is asked to open their parcel and look at the gift they have been given.

3. Ask the group to assemble their jigsaw. They will discover that a lot of pieces are missing. (While they are assembling the jigsaw get an assistant leader to hide some more parcels around the room with people's names on them.)

4. *Talk-to*:
'If we don't use all the gifts God has given us, the Church is like the picture, incomplete. Not everyone is using all their gifts. Some people have other gifts hidden around the room.'

5. Let them hunt out the other parcels. Those named on the parcels should open them and insert the pieces in the jigsaw. (Even with these pieces added the picture should not be complete!)

6. *Talk to*:
(i) Everyone has at least one spiritual gift, some people have more than one. (Explain that spiritual gifts are dierent from natural abilities.)
(ii) Sometimes it is easier for other people to identify our spiritual gifts (illustrate from the hunt round the room).
(iii) We must all use our gifts if the church is to work properly.
(iv) The less spectacular gifts are equally important for the functioning of the body (we can't all be outside pieces!).
(v) Round the talk o and answer any questions.

7. Pass out some more copies of the True or False question-

naire completed in the warm-up. Give everyone one minute to fill it in, then run through the answers. Collect the questionnaires in (so you can compare answers given before and after the activities).

8. Close in prayer.

Hints

Bible verses to help:

Gifts of the Spirit	*Fruit of the Spirit*	*General*
Ephesians 4:11	Galatians 5:22	Ephesians 1:13
1 Cor. 12:4–11		Galatians 5:16–18
1 Cor. 12:27–31		Romans 8
Romans 12:6–8		

Filled with the Spirit

Questionnaire

	True	*False*
The Holy Spirit is a person	☐	☐
The Holy Spirit is a feeling	☐	☐
There are many gifts of the Holy Spirit	☐	☐
There is only one fruit of the Spirit	☐	☐
The Holy Spirit is for Special Christians	☐	☐

The Holy Spirit brings power	☐	☐
Being filled with the Holy Spirit is a once-only experience	☐	☐

Filled with the Spirit

Discussion Starters

1. Each person name one thing they found helpful in the illustration of the coffee pot.
2. What does the lid represent to you:
   (a) as an individual?
   (b) as a group?
3. What two things can each of us do today to make us more open to the Holy Spirit?
4. What could we do similarly as a group?

Homosexual partnership

Aim

To help the young people gain a biblical understanding of the issues involved in homosexual partnership.

Warm-up

1. Silent Organisation (from Section II) on birthdays.
2. Mirrors (from Section II).
3. Trust games (from Section II).

The warm-up is aimed at building a warm, friendly, trusting atmosphere in which people feel safe to share.

Preparation

Some background reading and a good understanding of the biblical principles yourself are needed. The leader must be sensitive to those in the group who may be attracted towards their own sex. Prepare instruction sheets – one for each group of four.

Main session

A. *Advertisements*

1. In pairs, everyone has to write an advertisement selling their partner. Let them use their imagination – it could be a jingle, a comparison to a car or washing powder, etc.

2. Put the advertisements in a heap in the middle and get people to pick one out in turn and guess who it describes.

B. *Brainstorm*
Write down all the words that come to mind when we hear the word 'homosexual'. Put the list up so that everyone can see.

C. *Talk-to*
What do we mean by a homosexual?

1. In God's eyes there is no such thing – there are only people created in God's image, for whom Jesus died.

2. Everyone's sexuality is on a sliding scale between homosexual and heterosexual.

3. Christianity prohibits *any* promiscuous lifestyle.

D. *Bible Study*
1. Give each group of four one of the passages below and a copy of the instructions.

(a) Genesis 19:1–13.
(b) Leviticus 18:22; 20:13.
(c) Romans 1:18–32.
(d) 1 Cor. 6:9–10; 1 Tim. 1:8–11.

Instructions

(a) Read the passage out loud twice, with two different readers (and two Bible versions if you have them).
(b) What is the passage about? (Who is it for, why was it written, etc.)
(c) What is God saying through the passage?
(d) How can we apply or learn from what God is saying to us?

2. Get each group in turn to tell the others what they have learnt.

E. *Talk-to*
Read Romans 3:10–18. Point out that everyone sins and there is not a table of worse and better sins.

Read Romans 3:22–26. Even though we have all sinned and fallen short, God will forgive us if we turn to him.

Conclusion

Someone once said: 'Love the sinner, hate the sin.' All too often we hate the sinner and love our sin. The Bible clearly forbids homosexual partnerships, as it does any sexual relationships outside marriage, but as Christians we need to give a loving, Christian response.

What makes a Christian?

Aim

To make the young people think about preconceptions and stereotypes of Christians and what being a Christian is really about.

Equipment

Pens, big sheets of paper.

Preparation

Questionnaires and For Study sheets – one for each person.

Main session

1. On a large sheet, draw an archetypal Christian (either drawing it yourself with suggestions from the group, or getting the young people to do it). Take about 20 minutes.

2. Give out the questionnaire, and get each person to fill it in. Compare answers.

3. Hand out the 'For Study' sheets. Use them as a verse-look-up competition, or produce the verses on cards. Suggest they take the sheets home for further study.

Questionnaire

What is a Christian? Look at these statements and write True or False beside each one.

You are a Christian if . . .

1. You were born in England . . . . . .
2. You go to church . . . . . .
3. You eat wholefoods . . . . . .
4. You do not drink alcohol . . . . . .
5. You never go out with members of the opposite sex . . . . . .
6. You read the Bible . . . . . .
7. You like Cliff Richard . . . . . .
8. You pray all day . . . . . .
9. You do good things . . . . . .
10. You are always religious . . . . . .
11. You love your next-door neighbours . . . . . .
12. You have been christened . . . . . .

For Study

Look up these verses in the Bible when you have time to think about them.

John 6:35	John 14:21
John 7:37, 38	John 14:23
John 8:12	Romans 3:22–24
John 10:27–29	Romans 10:9–11
John 11:25, 26	

Other Bible references:

1.	Matt 28:19	–	make disciples of all nations.
	Acts 1:8	–	you will be my witnesses . . . to the ends of the earth.
2.	Matt 7:21	–	not everyone who calls me 'Lord, Lord . . .'
3.	Acts 10:15	–	do not consider unclean anything God has declared clean.
4.	John 2:10	–	water into wine.
	Matt 26:27	–	last supper.
5.	Eph 5:31	–	marriage.
6.	Matt 5:20	–	be more faithful than teachers of law and Pharisees.
7.	Exod 20:3	–	you shall have no other gods before me.
8.	Luke 18:10	–	Pharisee praying.
9.	Eccles 17:20	–	no one is good all the time.
10.	Eph 2:9	–	saved by grace, not good works.
11.	Luke 12:43	–	Pharisees in church.
12.	Rom 11:1	–	Paul, a Jew of Jews.

Prayer paths

Aim

To help the young people understand more about prayer.

Warm-up

1. Colour Clash (from Section II).
2. Talk Down (from Section II).

Main session

1. Person A talks to a partner (B) for one minute about what he/she has done over this last week, and the partner must listen without interrupting.

2. Swap over so that the listening partner (B) now has a chance to speak for one minute on what he/she has done in the last week and Person A does the listening.

3. B now has to tell A all that A has done in the past week.

4. A has to tell B all that B has done in the past week.

5. Quickly debrief: Which was easier – talking or listening? Why was talking easier?

Talk-to:
Today we are looking at prayer. Prayer involves not just talking to God, but also listening to him speaking to us. Before we look at what we mean by talking and listening to God, let us try and identify *our own* understanding of prayer.

Give out the Prayer Exploration sheets for each person to fill in. Then briefly get people to share what they've put, e.g. hands up all who circled (a) for the first question.

Prayer is communication with God. How do we communicate with each other? Brainstorm for one minute – answers will include speaking, touching, writing, hearing, reading, actions, signs . . . Just as we have different ways of communicating with each other, there are different types of prayer.

We are going to use the different types of prayer to build a Prayer Path. (If you can get five paving slabs and label them P,A,T,H & S that would be great – if not five large card squares similarly labelled would do. Lay out the squares one at a time in front of the group.)

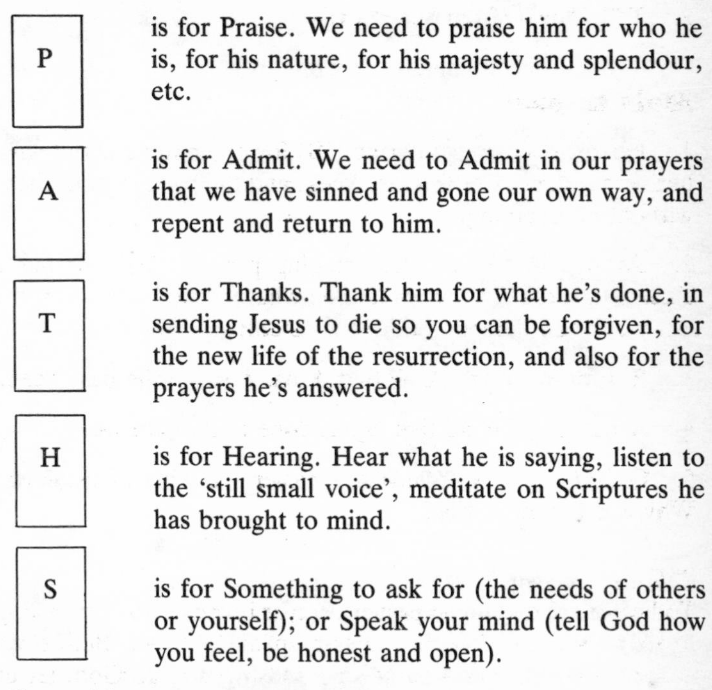

P is for Praise. We need to praise him for who he is, for his nature, for his majesty and splendour, etc.

A is for Admit. We need to Admit in our prayers that we have sinned and gone our own way, and repent and return to him.

T is for Thanks. Thank him for what he's done, in sending Jesus to die so you can be forgiven, for the new life of the resurrection, and also for the prayers he's answered.

H is for Hearing. Hear what he is saying, listen to the 'still small voice', meditate on Scriptures he has brought to mind.

S is for Something to ask for (the needs of others or yourself); or Speak your mind (tell God how you feel, be honest and open).

Close with prayer, or go on to:

Going Further

Divide the group into five and give them one card per group.

1. *Praise*
   Psalm 7:17
   Psalm 60

2. *Admit*
   Luke 11:4
   Psalm 51

3. *Thanks*
   Philippians 1:3–4
   Philippians 4:6
   Psalms

4. *Hear*
   1 John 5:14

5. *Speak*
   Psalm 99:6
   Jer. 15:1
   1 Sam 7:8–9

Each group has 10 minutes to prepare a short prayer time based on their type of prayer, appropriate to the group. After 10 minutes bring the groups back together and let them lead through their prayers, then close with the Lord's Prayer.

Prayer Exploration

Circle your opinions

Prayer is:
- (a) talking to yourself.
- (b) only for old people.
- (c) communication with God.
- (d) a waste of time.
- (e) only done in church.

When we pray to God:
- (a) he ignores us completely.
- (b) we switch off our brains.
- (c) we build up a relationship.
- (d) we have to have our eyes closed.
- (e) he will answer either Yes, No or Wait.

Put an X on the line
I find prayer:
boring _ exciting
easy _ difficult
morning activity _ _ _ _ _ _ _ _ _ _ _ _ _ evening activity
easy with friends _ _ _ _ _ _ _ _ _ _ _ _ _ easy by myself

Rate 1–10 (1 = not important, 10 = very important for you)

Daily prayer time ______

Panic prayers ______

Church prayer ______

Youth group prayer ______

Jekyll and Hyde

Aim

To help the young people to recognise the source of temptation and how to deal with it.

Warm-up

Use a few drama starters and lively warm-ups.

Main session

1. Everyone needs to have a partner, then:

2. Divide into groups of four people (or six if there is an odd number of pairs). Each pair acts the part of one person; one is the person speaking, and the other is that person's thoughts. Act out some of these situations:

   (a) After a very late night out John comes down to breakfast and has to face his mother's questions.

   (b) At school you are left in the changing room with a girl you are sure stole your pen the week before.

   (c) You stay too late at the youth meeting, miss your bus, arrive home an hour late, and your father is waiting at the door.

3. Get the group back together and briefly discuss what happened.

4. Divide into threes: (i) the *person*, (ii) *conscience*, (iii) *temptation*. As before, act out situations:

   (a) You go out to the pub with your boy/girlfrend and you are under eighteen.

(b) You have been told to tidy your bedroom, but you have just been bought a new set of headphones.
(c) You don't want to do P.E. so you leave your kit at home, and the games teacher asks you why you haven't got it.
(d) Choose your own situation on your own or in a large group.

5. Come back together as a group and discuss the following:
   (a) How did we feel: (i) conscience, (ii) temptation, (iii) person?
   (b) How true was this to your own experience in life?
   (c) How do we deal (i) with our conscience, (ii) with temptation?

Conclusion

If you are a Christian, what resources can you call on to help you deal with temptation?

Talk about the power of the Holy Spirit within our lives.

Agony Aunt evening

Aim

To understand personal problems and to consider what may be the Christian answer.

Warm-up

Divide the group into fours. Ask them to describe to other members in turn, firstly, the best thing that ever happened to them and, secondly, the worst thing that ever happened.

Preparation

Over the preceding weeks collect together as many problem pages as possible from various magazines. Then make a careful selection of the type of problems which your teenagers could relate to and which you want them to consider, e.g. family relationships, boy/girl partnerships, sex, honesty, personal integrity, guilt, etc.

Main session

1. Divide into groups. According to how your young people relate to each other, you may consider it appropriate to have groups of four, or larger, or indeed to stay in one large group.

2. Give each group three of the problem letters. You can give each group the same letters or different ones. Do not give them the Agony Aunt's reply. Ask each group to discuss what advice they would give in answer to each problem. Allow around fifteen minutes.

3. Bring everybody together and ask each group to read out one of their problems and the advice they would give. Then open the issue up for discussion generally. You may like to draw together the salient points and mention any distinctive Christian understanding of the problem. Then it may be appropriate to read out and discuss the answer which the Agony Aunt gave.

4. Go through the three problems of each group or, if time is short, take just one problem from each.

Conclusion

It is helpful for teenagers to appreciate the various perspectives on their own and other people's personal problems. This activity will encourage them to talk frankly and openly about sensitive subjects. It should also be an opportunity to do some teaching on Christian ethics.

Some of the issues may strike an emotional chord, so be sensitive to provide opportunity for personal conversation with individuals when the main session is over.

The belief game

Aim

To stimulate the exchange of beliefs and attitudes within a secure environment and to build on the positive aspects of individuals' beliefs.

Preparation

You will need a pen, a piece of card and a sheet of paper for everyone. Each person's card can be identified either by using a different colour, or by asking them to write their name on it.

Main session

This activity works best with a group of older teenagers who know each other well, and are prepared to share their beliefs.

1. Get everyone to sit on the floor in a circle. Then ask them to write on their sheet of paper a statement of their choice about something which they strongly believe. Allow them some time to think about this and perhaps make some suggestions, e.g. marriage, sex, work, moral standards, God, the Church, the future, the government, etc. Each person must write down a statement which begins 'I believe . . .'

2. Choose someone to be the first person to begin the game. Ask this person to place his or her statement of belief in the centre of the circle. Then ask all the others to place their card close to or far from the statement of belief, accordng to how much they agree with it. For example, if they agree totally they

can place it beside the statement, and if they totally disagree they can place it on the edge of the circle of people.

3. Ask the person to explain why he or she believes in the statement. Then ask those who have placed their cards near or far from the statement why they agree or disagree. You can have some lively and stimulating discussions throughout the evening.

Hints

It is important for you as chairperson not to intervene and correct what you may believe is wrong, but rather to allow the variety of views in the group to be expressed and respected. With some statements there may be very little discussion, which is fine. You also need to be aware when someone is making a statement just to be provocative.

This can be a very constructive evening and can give you as leader a valuable insight into what your young people really believe – which you may want to take into account when planning the teaching content of your next programe.

The Gulag Gospel

Aim

To help the teenagers understand something of living under an anti-Christian régime, and also find out how well they know their Bible.

Equipment

Pen and paper for each group.
Flipchart or overhead projector.

Preparation

Get in touch with Amnesty International and ask for details of Christians who are persecuted for their faith. You may wish to ask for a particular country. Amnesty's regular magazine has a Church section which reports on those Christians imprisoned for their faith. It is helpful if you can talk about individual cases of persecution, pass around photographs showing cases of harassment or victimisation. In fact use anything which will make the subject more real – photos, letters, newspaper articles, slides, a video, etc.

Main session

1. When the group gets together, confiscate all Bibles. (This may not be a problem if your teenagers are not in the habit of bringing theirs along!) Then ask them to imagine that they live in a country which is hostile to Christians and actively persecuting believers. Because of their faith they are sentenced

to a labour camp, and are not allowed to take any of their personal belongings.

2. Put everyone into small groups (pairs or fours), and provide each group with pen and paper. Tell them that they are a group of Christians in the labour camp, all Bibles and religious literature have been confiscated, and they have to see how much of the Bible they can remember and write down as accurately as possible. But before they scream, 'That's impossible,' ask them if they can remember some of the key events of the Gospel. Using the overhead projector or flipchart, note them down under the categories of parables, miracles, teaching, significant events.

3. Ask each group to choose one of the suggested incidents or stories and write it down as accurately as they can remember. Give them about 10–15 minutes for this, then ask each group in turn to read out what they have written. The other groups can contribute if they wish.

4. When each group has had its turn, see if you can arrange the events in chronological order.

Talk-to:
There is a multitude of issues for teaching arising out of the Gulag Gospel. You could talk about the importance of the Bible, its nature and historical background, what it reveals to us of God; also of the importance of the help and support that other believers can give by their knowledge of God and the Bible. You might find this session very revealing on how much both teenagers and leaders know or don't know of the Bible.

Question time

Aim

To promote discussion and awareness on teenage issues.

Equipment

Table, chairs and possibly microphones.

Preparation

1. Decide first of all how you are going to stage the evening. You could cover one particular topic such as parents, school, relationships, being a Christian, or you could have a general question time tackling a range of issues.

2. About a month beforehand get the young people involved in the preparation, perhaps at the end of a youth group meeting. Give them a pen and paper and allow them five minutes to write down a question relating to the topic you have chosen, or any general question which they wish to raise with a panel.

The advantage of doing things this way is that it means you receive questions from the majority of the group, not just a few; you have plenty of time to sort out the sensible and super questions; and you give the panel time to prepare a well-considered answer.

3. Now decide on the panel. You could have four mature teenagers, or four teenagers and four adults, or two teenagers and two parents, or two teenagers and two members of the P.C.C. Give it serious thought and be imaginative. One youth group invited their local M.P. and he agreed to come. It proved to be a very successful evening and it gave encouragement and recognition to the youth group.

Main session

1. Most of the work is done in the preparation. When you come to the main session give some thought to how you execute the event. For example, will the chairperson and the panel sit behind a table and give the event a serious official look, which may be the atmosphere you hope to create? On the other hand, you could seat the panel on easy chairs and create the informal atmosphere of a living room. With a large youth group and a formal approach, you could use microphones to give a more professional finish.

2. Choose a capable chairperson who can field questions and answers in an acceptable manner. Chairing a meeting successfully is quite an art. If you decide to ask one of the teenagers, look for someone who can keep discipline and is confident in their manner. Also don't forget a chairperson is supposed to be impartial.

3. If the event is thoughtfully managed, there should be a lot of good teaching coming out of the panel's comments and also some valuable views and contributions from the floor.

Hints

When the young people are thinking up their questions, it may be helpful to provoke some ideas. As well as the many issues of faith and being a Christian, you might consider Sunday trading, racial discrimination, animal vivisection, unemployment, the environment, abortion, pre-marital sex, etc.

Sanctification Star

Aim

To help the young people to see the influence of Jesus Christ on their lives and to pinpoint areas of their life that need to open to change.

Warm-up

A time of praise and worship.

Equipment

Felt pens for colouring and enough copies of the Sanctification Star for one each plus a few left over.

Main session

1. Give everyone a copy of the Sanctification Star.

2. Ask them to mark each of their spokes with a cross to indicate where they are on that issue, e.g. if someone prays only occasionally, put a cross on the Prayer line at 'occasionally'.

3. When they have done this for every one of the issues, ask them to draw connecting lines between the crosses and colour in the area between the centre circle and their line.

4. When they have coloured it in, ask them to change the colour of their pen and to put crosses on the line to indicate their position before they became Christians (or, if they have been a Christian a long time, where they were two or three years ago).

5. Now ask them to draw a circle running concentrically to the middle circle. Starting at the Patience line at the point 'with people I do not like', the line should run through 'regularly . . . I'll be kind if I must . . . weekly (but bored) . . . (Time) 10% . . . (Money) 10%' . . .'

6. Ask everyone to share about how they have changed, which areas have shown most improvement, etc.

Talk-to
Explain that the concentric circle they have drawn shows the minimum requirement of a Christian. Those areas that lie outside it need to be given up to God.

This should lead to some heated discussion on the cost of being a Christian. After everyone has had an opportunity to speak, conclude that the evidence shows God's Holy Spirit changing people and that if we open ourselves to his transforming power we can continue to change.

Conclusion

Sing 'Jesus, take me as I am', or something similar.

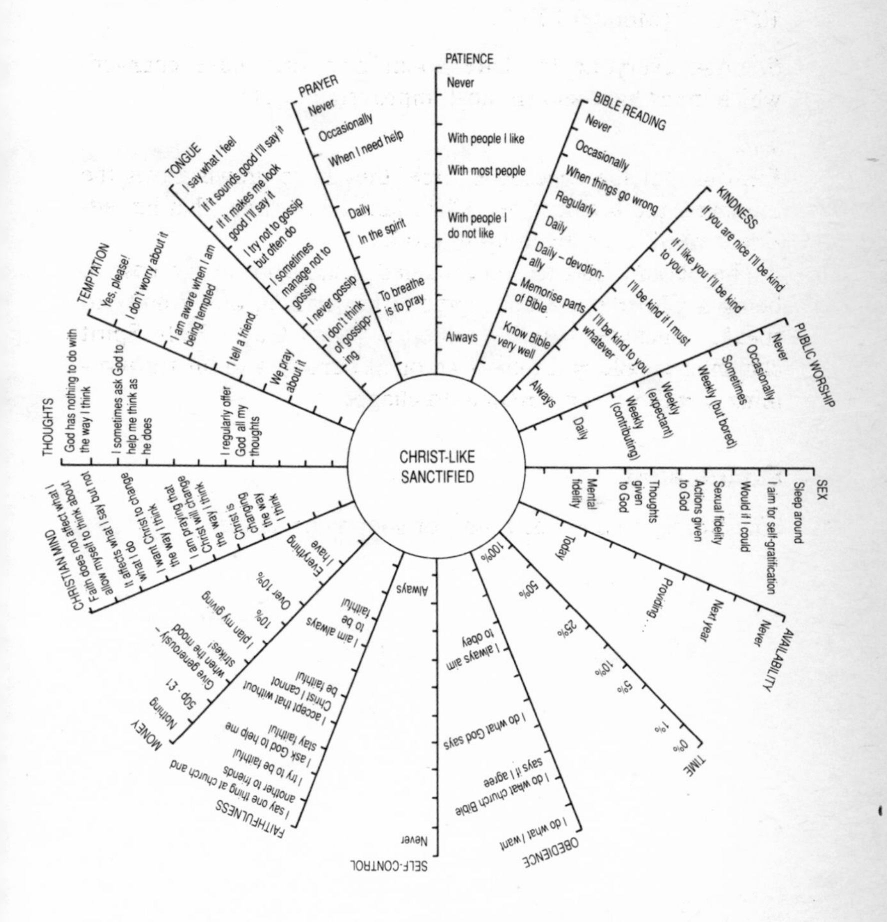
CHRIST-LIKE
SANCTIFIED
PATIENCE
Never
With people I like
With most people
With people I do not like
Always
BIBLE READING
Never
Occasionally
When things go wrong
Regularly
Daily
Daily – devotionally
Memorise parts of Bible
Know Bible very well
KINDNESS
If you are nice I'll be kind
If I like you I'll be kind to you
I'll be kind if I must
I'll be kind to you whatever
Always
PUBLIC WORSHIP
Never
Occasionally
Sometimes
Weekly (but bored)
Weekly (expectant)
Weekly (contributing)
Daily
SEX
Sleep around
I aim for self-gratification
Would if I could
Sexual fidelity
Actions given to God
Thoughts given to God
Mental fidelity
AVAILABILITY
Never
Next year
Providing . . .
Today
TIME
0%
1%
5%
10%
25%
50%
100%
OBEDIENCE
I do what I want
I do what church Bible says if I agree
I do what God says
I always aim to obey
SELF-CONTROL
Never
Always
FAITHFULNESS
I say one thing at church and another to friends
I try to be faithful
I ask God to help me stay faithful
I accept that without Christ I cannot be faithful
I aim always to be faithful
MONEY
Nothing
50p - £1
Give generously – when the mood strikes!
I plan my giving
10%
Over 10%
Everything I have
CHRISTIAN MIND
Faith does not affect what I allow myself to think about
It affects what I say but not what I do
I want Christ to change the way I think
I am praying that Christ will change the way I think
Christ is changing the way I think
THOUGHTS
God has nothing to do with the way I think
I sometimes ask God to help me think as he does
I regularly offer God all my thoughts
TEMPTATION
Yes, please!
I don't worry about it
I am aware when I am being tempted
I tell a friend
We pray about it
TONGUE
I say what I feel
If it sounds good I'll say it
If it makes me look good I'll say it
I try not to gossip but often do
I sometimes manage not to gossip
I never gossip
I don't think of gossipping
PRAYER
Never
Occasionally
When I need help
Daily
In the spirit
To breathe is to pray

Time to serve Christ

Aim

To provoke young people to consider whether God may be calling them to serve the Church, and to assist them in discovering his plan for their life.

Equipment

Pencils, questionnaires – one each. OHP or flipchart.

Main session

1. Give each person a questionnaire to fill in.

2. Get the group to discuss what people chose to tick. Why did they favour certain activities and not others?

3. Discuss what they feel are the most important activities. Are they necessarily the easiest to perform?

4. What gifts and skills would be needed to accomplish what they consider to be the most important activities? (You might want to use an OHP or flipchart.)

Talk-to

1. Look together at Exodus 3:1–12 and Isaiah 6:1–8. Why did Moses and Isaiah feel inadequate? Each had his own reasons. But what do you think made them succeed at the task God had given to them?

2. Next look together at Matthew 9:35–38. There is an urgent need today for workers in God's Church. We have seen how

God called Moses and Isaiah, but how do you think he calls people today to serve him?

(At this point you may wish to interview one of your church leaders or someone who has been called to serve the church in some way).

3. How do we hear God's call? Look at Acts 13:1–3. The church at Antioch discovered God's will for Saul and Barnabas by prayer and fasting. If we want to discover God's purposes and plan for our lives, we too must pray and at times fast. But there are some other important things we can do as well:

(a) Discuss with our friends any ideas we may have of what God wants us to do.
(b) Discuss your thoughts with a church or youth group leader.
(c) Develop your gifts and skills by using them to serve others in whatever way you can.
(d) Learn more about your faith and let your trust in God grow and flourish.
(e) Draw your spiritual strength from your personal devotional times as well as the church's worship and especially Holy Communion.
(f) Express your love for God and people in practical ways.

Questionnaire

If you had the opportunity to help the church in some way, what would you like to do? Tick as many as you wish.

1. Read a lesson.............
2. Clean the brass............
3. Visit the elderly..........
4. Preach a sermon.........
5. Take a school assembly
6. Help with Sunday school
7. Visit someone in hospital
8. Help lead a housegroup
18. Arrange the flowers......
19. Explain to someone what it means to be a Christian...................
20. Take a marriage service
21. Sing in the choir..........
22. Look after the church boiler........................

9. Support someone with a problem ....
10. Lead a service ....
11. Read the prayers ....
12. Sit on the PCC/eldership
13. Cut the grass in the churchyard ....
14. Join a drama group ......
15. Assist with a funeral.....
16. Baptise a baby ....
17. Chair a committee meeting.....................
23. Encourage people to give their money to the church ....
24. Arrange for someone to fix the leak in the church roof...........................
25. Support the activities of the church by your prayers
26. Promote concern for political and social issues
27. Study the doctrines of the Christian faith........

Video star

Aim

To promote a deeper understanding of faith. To provide an opportunity to develop camera/video skills.

Preparation

1. Hire a video camera and tripod from the local youth oce of the County Council. Or borrow an insured camera from a member of the congregation or a hire shop.

2. If you have a small group you can divide them into two teams. With a large number, divide into groups of four.

3. Your aim is to produce a programme of no longer than 30 minutes, in which members of the congregation are interviewed about their Christian faith. Each team is to visit and interview one person at home one evening in the week.

4. The young people should be allowed to prepare and run the interview themselves and to choose their own questions. However, stress that all the interviews should be within a strict time limit.

5. Before each team goes out they need to be briefed on how to operate the equipment, etc.

Main session

At your next youth group meeting, replay the videotape of the interviews. Obviously the response from the teenagers will be quite passive since it is a question of listening to other people talk of their faith in God.

If you wish to add a light-hearted aspect to the evening you could begin with coffee and as people arrive interview them about what faith in God means to them. Some will give you a serious reply; some will be thrown by the queston and the fact that it is on video. You could replay this at the end of the evening.

Variations

You could interview people on a whole range of issues such as guidance, prayer, etc. Or you could interview shoppers in your local High Street one Saturday morning on their views of God.

Open to God

Aim

To expand awareness of the ways in which God communicates with us.

Equipment

Blindfolds, lots of household items (see below), Bibles.

Main session

1. In this activity we will be asking the young people to experience the three senses of taste, smell and touch. Encourage as many as possible to participate. So ask about a third of the group to volunteer for the first experience of taste. Blindfold them, and arrange about ten items for tasting, e.g. jam, baked beans, cold tea, bread, rice, butter, etc. For entertainment value make sure this is done in the full view of all the group, and keep a record of who gets the right answer.

2. For the second part try smell. Again use items from your kitchen, e.g. mustard, Marmite, HP sauce, garlic, vinegar, etc.

3. Finally your third group is asked to identify by touch. So collect together a number of household items which are not easily identifiable by touch. Once everyone has finished it may be worth mentioning who got the most items right.

4. As an extra event, ask three volunteers to be blindfolded and lie on the floor on their backs. Then ask six people to stand three on either side of them. The three on the left side should link their hands underneath the person on the floor with

those standing opposite. Each group should then lift the person in the air. At various points they should ask how high the person thinks he or she is off the ground. (This activity is fun to do but has only vague links with touch and trust. Leave it out if you prefer.)

5. Distribute Bibles and look together at Psalm 34:8 and John 7:37. Discuss:

(a) In what ways can you 'taste' and see how good God is? What does it mean? Make a list of their ideas.
(b) What type of thirst is Jesus talking about and how does this thirst exhibit itself? How do you drink from Jesus? What does it mean in practice?
(c) What other levels of perception do we have as humans apart from taste, smell and touch?

Forgive and Forget

Aim

To explore the issue of forgiveness in human relationships.

Equipment

Pens, Bibles – one each.

Preparation

Prepare enough worksheets for the group to have one each.

Main session

1. Ask each person to fill in the worksheet:

Forgiveness factor

Mark each situation below on a scale of 0–3 to show whether you feel they are easy or difficult to forgive (0 = not a problem; 3 = almost unforgivable).

- Changing TV channels when I'm watching my favourite programme
- Betraying my confidence
- Not turning up for an appointment
- Scratching my best record album
- Borrowing something important and not returning it
- Being ignored by a friend
- Stealing one of my possessions
- Unjustly being called a liar

- Being called unpleasant nicknames
- Spreading false rumours about me
- One of my parents wanting a divorce
- Parents blaming me for something I did not do

2. When everyone has filled in the sheet, go through each issue and allow a discussion to develop. Listen to what the young people are saying and give them plenty of opportunity to express their views.

3. Give out Bibles and look together at Matthew 18:21–35. Discuss the following questions:
   (a) What do you think motivated Peter to ask this question?
   (b) Do you think Jesus literally meant seventy times seven?
   (c) Was Jesus being realistic?
   (d) When someone has really hurt you what is your normal reaction?
   (e) What should our reaction be in the light of this parable?

4. Then look at Luke 23:26–34. What is the whole point of the example of Jesus when we are faced with the need to forgive?

5. Close with a meditation on the Cross. Ask the group to be quiet and still and then gently ask them to picture the scene from Luke's Gospel. Give them plenty of time to paint the scene in their own minds. Carefully in a sentence or two mention the blood, the sweat, the agony and the intense heat of the scene at Golgotha. The idea is for them to see the scene in all its horror for themselves. When the time is right ask them to leave the scene with the tortured Jesus uttering the words, 'Father, forgive them, for they do not know what they are doing.' Close by saying the Grace together.

SECTION V

GROUPBUILDERS

Bread and wine

Aim

To devise your own service of Breaking of Bread involving all members of the group.

Preparation

You will need musical instruments, candles, bread, wine, pen, paper, Bibles, songbooks and orders of service books – A.S.B. for example.

Main session

This can be a very powerful group activity and can be particularly helpful at the beginning or end of a term's programme.

There are a number of constituent parts of a Communion service which groups of young people can organise, for example, reading, drama, dance, Peace, prayers, liturgy and music. You do not have to use all of these – choose the items which fit in with your usual manner of Breaking Bread and which are appropriate to the gifts of your group.

Discuss with the group what theme they would like to follow. Then move into action on the other parts of the service. Don't try to do to much. Keep it simple.

For example, you could divide them into three groups: one to select and rehearse the music, another to choose and prepare the readings and another to rewrite some of the liturgy. The first two areas are obvious; with the liturgy you could ask them to rewrite the prayer of Humble Access or the Confession or

Thanksgiving. Get them to express it in a way that relates to them. Give them an hour to prepare and rehearse.

Before you begin the service bring all the groups back together again and weave together their ideas into an order of service. If you are having a proper Communion then in some churches you will need a priest. You may wish simply to have a Breaking of Bread and could read 1 Cor. 2:23–26 before you pass the bread and wine around. With a little imagination it is possible to put together a very relevant and meaningful act of worship. If you all sit in a circle you can place a small table in the centre with a couple of candles on it if you so desire. You can use silence during the service as well. The important thing is to get everyone involved.

Below is an example of an order of service, but of course you can arrange things in whatever manner you wish! It is best to allow at least one and a half hours for the preparation and service.

1. Songs (two or three)
2. Reading
3. Drama
4. Songs
5. Peace
6. Confession and Prayer of Humble Access
7. Songs
8. Breaking of Bread
9. Dance
10. Final song.

Youth review

Aim

To have fun and to promote the identity of the youth work in the church.

Preparation

The idea is to hold a Youth Review. It can be carried out in a variety of ways:

1. You can ask various members of your group to get together to produce a presentation of 5–10 minutes. Even with just 4 groups you have sufficient for a programme.

2. You can ask all the young people's groups in your church to present a 10-minute programme, e.g. the choir, Brownies, Guides, Cubs, Scouts, Boys' Brigade, servers, bell-ringers and youth groups. This can be a very positive event, promoting unity and understanding.

3. You can do an area event involving all the local youth groups.

Obvious decisions you will have to make are where and when the Youth Review will take place and who it is for. You may want it to be simply for the entertainment of the young people, or you may want it to be for the parents. In one church they decided to invite the parents of the various members of the youth organisations and made a small charge, raising £120 for charity.

You will need one person to co-ordinate all the activities to make sure that there is no duplication in the programme. Then you will need a gifted individual to compère the event on the night.

Main session

Most of the work will be in the preparation of the event. Depending on your audience you can present a programme of anything from 30 minutes to 1 hour 15 minutes.

Hints

Prepare well in advance. Make sure you have extensive consultation and involvement.

Love is . . .

Aim

To promote openness and a deeper sense of care and fellowship. (N.B. This activity needs to be handled with great care and sensitivity and within a positive atmosphere.)

Warm-up

Play a couple of icebreakers which people will enjoy and which will make them feel positive.

Preparation

Pens, paper and New Testaments – one for each member.

Main session

1. Give each member a pen and paper, and ask them *not* to put their names on it and *not* to let anyone else see what they are writing. Then ask them to answer these questions, giving only a one-sentence answer.

   (a) The best thing about this group is . . .
   (b) The worst thing about this group is . . .
   (c) Describe your relationship with the member you get on with best.
   (d) Describe your relationship with the member you get on with least well.

2. When everyone has written their replies gather them all in, then read out the replies. This needs to be handled with

care and sensitivity. Judge when it is appropriate to encourage discussion on a point someone has made, and when you should pass on to the next comment.

3. Break into groups of about six people with a leader to each group. Hand out the New Testaments and ask one of the teenagers to read out 1 Corinthians 13. Bearing in mind the comments and replies to the first part of the evening, use this reading as the basis for a discussion of these questions:

(a) Why is love the most important and eternal virtue?

(b) Looking at the list of what love is, how does love relate to the everyday hassles of life, when you are dealing with difficult people at home, at school and in the youth group?

(c) Is this passage realistic in expecting us as individuals to practise this kind of love?

(d) How can we promote a greater degree of love and friendship within the group?

4. Taking one of the comments about one of the worst aspects of the youth group, leave the group for up to fifteen minutes to work out a simple role-play or sketch showing the most positive way to solve the problem. Then allow each group to present their role-play or drama to the others.

5. Finish by singing together suitable songs which stress love and understanding such as 'Bind us together'. Then share the 'Peace' together. Finally, choose an icebreaker that involves everyone and finish on a positive note.

Hints

Take care to follow up any comments which reveal a pastoral need. You may need to spend a week or two taking care of some of the issues raised during this session.

Bring a thing

Aim

To foster a sense of sharing and mutual understanding.

Warm-up

Play a few icebreakers, particularly ones that involve physical contact but do not produce high spirits.

Preparation

This simple activity can produce a very good evening which can do a lot to strengthen the group as a whole. A month ahead, begin encouraging the young people to think of an item that is important to them. It can be anything! Mention it each week and stress two things: *everyone* has to bring something, and they should be prepared to explain why the item is special to them. For the evening itself you will need a tape-recorder, record-player, a slide-projector and screen, and a hat containing folded and numbered pieces of paper (one piece for each person).

Main session

After coffee and a few icebreakers to help people relax, sit them down in a circle on the floor. Then pass the hat around containing the numbers. When everyone has drawn a number you then have the order in which they are going to speak about their 'thing'. You may find the range of 'things' people bring along is quite diverse – medals, certificates, photographs, slides, poems, a piece of music, a soft toy, a computer magazine, etc. You can find out some very interesting things about members of the group. Leaders, of course, have to participate as well. It is important to keep an eye on the time so that everyone has an opportunity to talk about their 'thing'.

Conclusion

Finish by having a time of prayer for each member of the group. You can either divide people into pairs to pray for each other, or, if the teenagers feel comfortable about it, have a time of open prayer concentrating on the positive aspects of friendships within the group. Or you can simply get everyone to stand and hold hands and say the Grace together.

Hints

If you have a large group of more than about 25 it is probably worth breaking up into smaller groups of around a dozen. Otherwise your session may take all night!

Parents' event

Aim

To strengthen the youth group's own identity as well as consolidate its relationship with the parents.

Hints

Remember with any event that you run for the teenagers that there is always an unseen audience – parents. The group relies on the goodwill and trust of all the parents of the young people, so anything you can do to strengthen that link will be positive.

Preparation

What you choose to lay on for the evening can vary. Many groups have successfully laid on an entertainment evening. You need to organise what you are going to do, and decide on the degree of Christian content you want in the programme. It need take no more than 30 minutes, and might include:

poetry
literature reading
singing
musical presentation
drama
dance
prayers
slides of the year's activities, etc.

Send out invitations to all the parents of the youth group members at least six weeks in advance. You might consider decorating the hall. Arrange tables and chairs into groups. As parents arrive serve them with a glass of wine or cup of coffee. Have various nibbles available on the tables. If you are not showing slides of the various youth activities over the year then it might be an idea to have a display of all your events.

Main session

During the evening try to speak to as many parents as possible, particularly those you do not know. Finally, do not under-estimate how valuable this event can be.

Group profiles

Aim

To help the group to know its make-up and to provide a resource pool of information.

Warm-up

Some good mixing icebreakers, e.g. Body Dice or Clumping (both in Section II). End up with the group in about six teams.

Equipment

Paper (large and small sheets), pens, felt pens, rulers, coloured pins, notice board (soft board), large street map of the area (enlarged to A2), tape measure, weight.

Preparation

Write out instruction sheets for each team, as below.

Main session

Give each team an instruction sheet and tell them they have 45 minutes to do what it says. (For a small group reduce the time, for a large group increase it.) When all the teams have finished get them to present their information.

Group profile instruction sheets

Team A

You are to find the name, address and telephone number of every member of the group.

Put a pin in the street map for their house. Label this pin with a number and write the number and corresponding details round the outside of the map.

Team B

You are to investigate the age/sex profile of the group and present the information on A2 paper to the group.

Then discover which schools all the members go to and again choose a method of presenting the material on A2 paper.

Team C

You are to investigate the group's attitude towards God. Produce a questionnaire with Yes/No answers, e.g.

'Do you believe in God?'
'Have you been baptised?'

and put the results onto A2 paper.

Team D

You are looking at the physical aspects of the group. Measure height, weight, shoe size, hair colour, etc. and present to the whole group on A2 paper.

Team E

You are investigating the church-going habits of the group. Find out how many go to church, to which one and how often.

Plot and present the information on A2 paper.

Team F

You are investigating the group's social needs. Find out where people go out to, how often, how much TV they watch, etc., and present the information on A2 paper.

Jesus file

Aim

To discover how much the group knows about Jesus and to get them working together.

Equipment

Coloured duplicator paper, pens.

Warm-up

A few icebreakers.

Main session

1. Ask each person to write down from memory, on separate pieces of paper:

(a)	one thing that Jesus taught	(on yellow paper)
(b)	one miracle that Jesus performed	(on blue paper)
(c)	one person that Jesus met	(on green paper)
(d)	one fact about Jesus' life	(on pink paper)

2. When everyone has done this to the best of their ability, form them into pairs (preferably with someone they don't know well). If you have odd numbers, pair one up with a leader. They then have to choose the six facts about Jesus which they feel are most important and which must include at least one of each colour of paper. Collect in the discarded sheets.

3. Form the pairs into groups of six or eight people and tell them that from their information (i.e. their pieces of paper)

they have to build a 'Gospel' containing only fifteen (for groups of 8) or twelve (for groups of 6) pieces of information, with a minimum of two for each colour.

4. When the groups have done this ask a spokesperson from each group to read out what they have included and put it up on a flipchart.

5. *Talk-to*: When the Gospel writers wrote down the teaching, miracles and information about Jesus' life, they had to choose what to include and what not to include. That is why we have some things that Jesus did in some Gospels and not others (illustrate this from the flipchart and the Bible), whereas important things are in all the Gospels (again illustrate from the flipchart and the Bible).

What do you think was the most important thing Jesus did? He died on the cross and was raised again from the dead. That is why the Gospel writers spend so much space on the crucifixion and resurrection.

6. Close with an appropriate prayer.

Radio St Stephen's

Aim

To promote team spirit and communication within the group.

Warm-up

Not needed as this exercise is best done from cold.

Preparation

Prepare news items, using the examples given – an identical set for each team.

Main session

1. Split the group into two or more news teams, of between four and seven people, and explain to each that it is to produce a five-minute news programme to be broadcast on radio to everyone within a two-mile radius of St Stephen's, and to the morning congregation. The 'news' will be broadcast precisely on the hour, when a tape-recorder will be brought into the news room, switched on, and after five minutes exactly will be switched off.

2. Over a period of one hour give each news team the same news briefs at odd intervals. News should arrive throughout the hour, even during the last few minutes.

3. Tape the broadcast as explained in 1. above.

4. Bring the news teams together again and listen to all the programmes.

Conclusion

Discuss with the groups how they coped in the following areas:

(a) Communication, leadership, teamwork.
(b) Presentation, style, order, ranking, timing.
(c) Bias, accuracy, news and representation of the real world.
(d) Decision-making: what is news and what is not news?

Variation

Give the group only 45 minutes before producing a four-minute news broadcast.

Radio St Stephen's News Briefs

1. *National Train Strike*

Many commuters stayed at home. Roads crowded. No trains running. Local NUR spokesperson said, 'Industrial action will be repeated if no solution can be found.' Local MP called for both sides to go to arbitration service ACAS.

2. *Gorbachev in Hungary*

President of USSR, Mikhail Gorbachev, visits Hungary. Third stop on Comecon Country tour. Spoke out for more political freedom. Radical demonstrations unopposed by government forces. Gorbachev calls on West to cut interest rates on Third World loans.

3. *Andy & Fergie Due to Visit Hamblemere*

Visit planned for opening of new hospice. Fund-raising chairman for new 23-bed hospice says, 'We are delighted.' Local First and Middle school heads said children would have the afternoon off school to see the Prince and his wife.

4. *Planning Permission*

Last night's Borough Council Planning Committee meeting approved the controversial Sickle Mill Flats, to be built on one of the few remaining green areas in the town. The flats which will cost over £100,000 each are aimed at the young executive. Local opposition councillors called the plan disgraceful, and urged the Chairman of the Planning Committee to resign.

5. *Police Warning*
Off-licences and pubs are warned in a letter from the Chief Constable that the police are clamping down on under-age drinking, following the tragic death of a 15-year-old from the effects of excess alcohol.

6. *Latest News*
A fire at Hamblemere Museum last night caused £5,000 worth of damage. Fire Brigade are still at the scene. Local people helped rescue many treasures including the famous 15th-century map of the town.

7. *Robbery*
Smith & Woodwars electrical shop on East Street was broken into over the weekend. Back window smashed. Thief got away with two portable CD players.

8. *Robbery Update*
A local youth is helping police with their enquiries. A police spokesman said, 'An arrest is expected shortly.'

9. *Water Shortage*
The local Water Authority announced a ban on the use of hosepipes and urged consumers to reduce consumption following the hottest and dryest May and June on record. Reservoir levels were described as a cause for concern.

10. *Road Works*
Major disruption continues for road users. Gaspipe laying has moved into Church Road and traffic has had to be diverted via Junction Place. A Gas Board official said the work would last for the next two weeks.

11. *Swimming Pool Summer Opening*
After last month's opening of the new learner pool at Hamblemere Swimming Baths the manager announced the pool would

be open from 10.00–12.00 and 2.00–4.00 every day throughout the summer holiday.

12. *Unrest in China*
Student protests continued in many parts of China. Authorities have made hundreds of arrests. No official information from the Chinese Government.

13. *Accident*
Police seek witnesses to a hit-and-run accident. The accident occurred at 6.45 on Chase Lane, when a red Escort crashed into the side of Fiona Jones' VW Polo, causing extensive damage.

14. *Kittens Rescued*
Six kittens rescued from a council tip today when a council workman heard faint cries. The kittens, though dehydrated, are doing well.

15. *Fire Update*
Fire at Hamblemere Museum caused £50,000 of damage not £5,000.

16. *Church Fête*
Local church fête raised over £4,000 for missionary work in Nepal. Rev. Timothy Fletcher was delighted by local people's support of church misson.

17. *Weather*
Hot weather to continue. Maximum today 19°C. Minimum tonight 11°C. Long range forecast: dry and hot.

18. *Sport*
England at tea were 240 for 4 on the first day of the second Test. David Gower 92 not out.

Local athlete, Peter Fellows, selected for England in international match against West Germany.

Who slept during the sermon?

Aim

1. To get all the group to participate.
2. To establish leaders within the group.
3. To get the group oriented towards problem solving.

Preparation

Write each of the twenty clues on a separate piece of paper.

Main session

Give the group the following information (adapting the leadership titles to your group's church background):

> During a lengthy sermon by the Vicar, one of the churchwardens is noticed to be asleep. Twenty members of the congregation each gave the Vicar one piece of information concerning the suspect. Unfortunately the Vicar was unable to work out who was asleep. We have here all the information needed to find out who it was.

Who slept during the sermon?
Clues

1. The man in the black coat smiled.
2. The man in the blue coat sat behind the man in the black coat.
3. Mr Turner never frowned during sermons.
4. Mr Bouch never smiled during sermons.

5. Mr McWhirr would never wear black to church.
6. Mr Turner sat on the right of the man in the brown coat.
7. Mr McWhirr was always early for church.
8. Mr Bouch sat behind the man in the grey coat.
9. The man in the grey coat sat in front of the man in the blue coat.
10. The man in the grey coat listened throughout the sermon.
11. Mr Lumb had spilled coffee down his only grey coat and it was at the dry cleaners.
12. The man who frowned sat to the left of the man who slept.
13. The Vicar could never see those at the back from the pulpit.
14. The man who slept wore a hat.
15. The man who slept sat behind the man in grey.
16. Mr Turner wore his black coat only for funerals.
17. The man who slept sat on the right of the man in the brown coat.
18. Mr McWhirr sat behind the man in the grey suit.
19. The man in the black suit did not sit behind Mr Bouch.
20. Mr Bouch sat to the left of the man in the blue coat.

Rules

1. Everyone will be given a clue or clues.
2. No one can look at anyone else's clues.
3. The only way to share your clue is by speaking.
4. We will only tell you if the answer is right or wrong.

Solution

Blue	*Grey*
McWhirr SLEPT	Turner Listened
Brown	*Black*
Bouch Frowned	Lumb Smiled

When the group have solved the problem, discuss the following points:

1. Was a leader needed?
2. How was time lost?
3. Why was it least effective for everyone to talk at once?
4. What problems arose because some people did not present their clues?
5. How did some people ignore the clues of others?
6. Did anyone try to encourage everyone to give their clues?
7. Was everyone included in discussion?
8. Did anyone take over the discussion?

Group friendship sculpture

Aim

To help the young people understand where they are in relationship to their friends, or to look at spiritual supposition and snobbery, or to look at families or childhood.

Warm-up

Sharing games, e.g. 'One thing that's a lie' (from Section II).

Equipment

Pens and paper.

Main session

1. Ask for a volunteer to stand in the middle.

2. Ask those who are his/her friends to come and join him/her.

3. The volunteer is to position these friends according to the rules (given below).

4. When the volunteer has positioned the friends, ask all the group to note their position.

5. Then ask each of the friends in turn if they would like to move or to move anyone.

6. When all the friends have done this, ask the group who are watching to reposition the friends the way it appears to them from outside the friendship. (This can be far more honest than the friends often are.)

7. When this is done, review the major differences, e.g. was 'X' positioned here by 'Y', but over there by 'Z'? Let people share how they felt as well as what happened.

Hints

This method could be used to look at how we feel or felt:

as a child
in class
at home
in this group
at school

Handle this carefully as people may have emotional hurts in these areas.

You could ask someone to arrange the rest of the group to show how people are perceived spiritually:

Height	–	more spiritual/less spiritual
Facing	–	more time with God facing one way; less – facing the other way
Closer	–	more important
Further away	–	less important

Talk-to:
Talk about how things are not always what they seem, e.g. some people may look holy and not be (Jesus talking about the Pharisee and the tax collector); or how we need to be open and honest about our faith. Close in prayer.

Rules

1. The closer your friendship with people, the nearer they should stand to you.
2. The more of your attention they have, the more in front

of you they should be; and the less, the further behind they should be.

3. The more you look up to them, the taller they should be made (stand them on a chair). The more you look down on them, the smaller they should be.
4. The more of their attention you think you have, the more they should face towards you; and the less attention, the less they should face towards you.

SECTION VI
PEOPLEBUILDERS

Heroes and villains

Aim

To demonstrate that in Jesus Christ we discover how God intended people to live.

Warm-up

Find three or four extrovert members of the youth group to act out being heroes to the hero music and villains to the villain music. Get the group to decide who was the best.

Equipment

Lots of newspaper, tape-player etc., paper, pens.

Preparation

Tape some 'heroes' music and some 'villains' music (from TV, radio, etc.)

Main session

1. Tip the newspaper into a heap in the middle of the floor.

2. Everyone has to hunt through until they find someone in an article who they see as a hero and someone they see as a villain.

3. Then write the characteristics of the person they have chosen that make him or her a hero/villain.

4. Ask people to read out the names of their heroes and their characteristics, and state why they chose them.

5. Write the characteristics (but not the names of the people chosen) up on a flipchart under two headings: positive and negative.

6. *Talk-to*: Looking at the list on the flipchart, can we imagine someone with all the positive qualities and no negatives? Explain that Jesus was perfect, he had all the positive qualities but none of the negative, and that is what God intended us to be like when he created us. But we rebelled and are rebelling against God still. So he sent his Son to live a perfect life. The religious people crucified him, but God raised him to life. Today we don't just have the example of Jesus' life, we can also have the power to be like him by having the Holy Spirit within us.

7. Ask the group members to each write a positive and a negative characteristic of theirs on a piece of paper, and in a time of silent prayer to thank God for the positive and to ask his help with the negative.

8. Then close in prayer.

I am . . . You are . . .

Aim

To encourage the group members to express how they feel about each other, and to be open and honest about strengths and weaknesses.

Warm-up

If your group enjoys singing then some quiet worship songs or a Taizé chant would be good. If not, use a Christian meditation, or a relaxation exercise – something that will quieten them and turn their thoughts towards God.

Main session

1. Tape a piece of A4 paper to each person's back and give them each a soft pencil or felt pen.

2. Ask each person to write on the back of all the others one thing they like about them.

3. Sit round in a circle, remove the papers, and get everyone to read out their list. They should say, 'I am . . .' If they agree with what is written, or 'Someone says I am . . .' if they don't agree.

4. Spend a time of quiet reflecting on this.

5. Stick another piece of paper on everyone's backs, and ask the group to write one thing they dislike about each person on the sheet.

6. Sit round in a circle and again everyone reads their list,

saying, 'I am . . .' if they agree, or 'Someone says I am . . .' if they disagree.

7. Spend some time quietly reflecting.

8. Ask each person in turn how they feel.

9. Then ask the group to pray for each person, either quietly or aloud.

Hints

If the group is too large, break it down into smaller units and hold the session in different rooms.

If you do this exercise you need to be confident that the group can handle it, and you need to exercise the utmost care and sensitivity.

Happiest memories

Aim

To help the young people to share at a deeper level and to recognise 'God experiences' in their lives.

Warm-up

Some lively mixing icebreakers, e.g. Clumping, Zoom and Frogger (from Section II), that end with the young people well mixed and in groups of between four and seven.

Preparation

Write out a list of questions for each group leader. (See below.)

Main session

The leader reads out a question then each person in the group in turn answers it. When everyone has said something and those who want to say lots have had a decent chance, move on to the next question. The questions are:

1. Think back to when you were a child of seven. Can you think of a special place that made you feel wanted or gave you a sense of belonging? (Get each member to share where, what and how.)

2. Do you still get such feelings of belonging today? (Get each member to share where, what and how.)

3. Have you ever had an experience of God that produced

the same feelings? (Get each member to share where, what and how.)

4. Do you still get such experiences of God, or would you like to know how such experiences of God can become a reality?

Hints

Group leaders need to be sensitive and listen carefully to what is shared and to be honest about their own experiences. Once the group is talking and sharing the session can last longer than you may expect. As well as feelings of belonging, other activities or events that have produced good positive experiences can be used, e.g. holidays, favourite toys, etc.

Marathon race

Aim

To get young people to identify where they see themselves in the Christian life.

Preparation

'Running the Race' sheets – one for each person. (See below.)

Main session

1. Talk about the Christian life as a race. Using the example of a marathon race, explain some of the different positions people can be in.

2. Hand out the 'Running the Race' sheets.

3. Ask everyone to think about where they are in their spiritual life and to tick the appropriate box on the sheet. (They need to keep their answers secret at this stage.)

4. When everyone has done this divide into groups of five.

5. Give them the following instructions:

   (a) Do not tell anyone which box you ticked yet.
   (b) For each of the people in the group, put a tick where you think they are in their spiritual life.
   (c) Taking each person in the group in turn, everyone says where they have put that person and why. The person then says where he/she has put him/herself, and why.
   (d) Do this for each member of the group.

6. Bring the groups back together, and

   (a) Ask if there are any comments.
   (b) Ask how many people were put in a different place by their group.
   (c) Talk about your spiritual life in terms of the different positions on your sheet, what you found helpful and how you have grown as a Christian. Invite comments from committed Christians within the group if they too want to say how they have found things.

Running the Race

The Christian life has often been compared to a race. Paul writes in 2 Timothy 4:7, 'I have fought the good fight, I have finished the race. I have kept the faith.' In this exercise we will be thinking about where we are in our own Christian life and comparing it to a marathon. So, after thinking about where you are spiritually, tick the boxes beside the statements that best describe your position.

(a) *In the race:*

- ☐ Waiting at the start
- ☐ Running hard at the beginning
- ☐ Running hard well into the race
- ☐ Chugging along at your own pace
- ☐ Taking a breather
- ☐ Slowing down
- ☐ Given up
- ☐ Taken a wrong turn and lost your way

(b) *Spectating:*

- ☐ Always watch but never take part

☐ Just passing so take a look

☐ Would like to join in but don't know how

☐ Thinking about running but unsure

(c) *Officiating:*

☐ A race marshal, always there but not in the race

☐ The coach, giving advice, but not actually in the race

(d) *Other:*

Please describe your position below, if different.

Hedgehogs

Aim

To help the young people identify where they are in the group, in the church or in their spiritual life.

Equipment

Pens, copies of hedgehogs for everyone.

Main session

1. Divide them into small groups of 5–8 people and pass out a photocopy of the hedgehogs drawing.

2. Choose which area you are going to look at (e.g. their spiritual life) and ask everyone to choose the hedgehog that best represents where they are in their spiritual life and mark it with their initials. Everyone must do this without showing the rest of the group.

3. Ask each member of the group to identify where the rest of their small group are in their spiritual life in terms of the hedgehogs on the picture and to mark them with the person's initials.

4. When everyone has done this, let each person in turn say where they have put themselves and why and let the rest of the group say where they have put that person and why. Work round the whole group.

5. When everyone has shared where they are, ask them to say which hedgehog they would like to be and why.

6. Close with quiet prayer for each member of the group.

God our Friend

Aim

To stimulate the young people to consider the friendship that God offers to us and the implications of that friendship on our lives.

Preparation

You will need Bibles, pens and paper, and, if appropriate, copies of the questions and texts.

Main session

1. Divide the young people into three groups of roughly equal numbers. The ideal size would be six or seven in each group so make an extra group if you have large numbers.

2. Give each group one of the three sets of texts and questions and ask them to consider the questions in the light of the text. You should allow 20–30 minutes for the discussion and ask each group to appoint a spokesperson.

A. (i) Luke 15:11–32
(ii) 2 Corinthians 5:14–21
Q. By what means does God make us his friends?
Q. What do the passages teach us about the nature of God?
Q. How should we communicate God's friendship to others?

B. (i) Isaiah 58:3–12
(ii) Leviticus 19:33–34

(iii) Luke 22:24–27

Q. What does God want us to do with our friendship?

Q. How can we establish justice and righteousness in our world?

Q. In what ways can our youth group express friendship towards the outsider?

C. (i) Luke 6:27–38

(ii) Matthew 18:21–35

Q. How far should we go in our friendship with others? Is Jesus' command practical?

Q. What attitudes should we adopt that would reflect God's love?

Q. How important to friendship is forgiveness?

3. When the groups have finished ask each spokesperson to report back on what their group felt about the passages and what answers they would give to the questions. Using either a flip-chart or an overhead projector write down the answers in headings format, and highlight what are the most important lessons from the discussions.

4. Then go and play a few icebreakers which are in some way connected with the notion of friendship.

Give it away!

Aim

To encourage the young people to realise that being a Christian involves sharing their faith with their friends and family.

Preparation

You will need pens, paper, Bibles, and a worksheet for each member of the group.

Main session

Divide the group up into smaller groups of what you consider the optimum number for good discussion. Then hand out worksheets prepared from the ideas below.

Worksheet

1. Take a look at Matthew 28:18–20 and Mark 16:15–16. What did Jesus tell us to do?

2. Spend about ten minutes discussing these questions with the rest of your group:

   (a) Who has the nicest smile?
   (b) Who has the most well-thumbed Bible?
   (c) Who is the one who talks most?
   (d) Who looks the most religious?
   (e) Who has been a Christian the longest?
   (f) Who has passed a religious education exam?
   (g) Who is the most outward-going?

(h) Who became a Christian most recently?
(i) Who knows the most about God?

Now discuss this question: what are the most important qualifications for being able to tell others about God?

3. Individually look at the list below and tick what you think are the three reasons why you rarely talk to others about God.
. . . I don't want others to know I'm a Christian.
. . . They would not understand.
. . . I'm not sure I know enough answers to my friends' questions.
. . . I might be persecuted for what I believe.
. . . It's not the sort of thing you talk about.
. . . My actions speak louder than words.
. . . I might be labelled a 'Bible-basher'.
. . . I'm not really that bothered.
. . . I'm not a good enough Christian.
Then discuss with your group the ones you have ticked and why you have ticked them.

4. Take a look at 1 Peter 3:15–6. Discuss these questions:

(a) What does it mean by the 'hope' you have as a Christian?
(b) What are the implications of honouring Jesus as the Lord of your life?
(c) In what ways do you feel your conduct may help or indeed hinder some people in finding God?

5. Finally get together in pairs and take it in turns to explain as clearly as you can what a Christian is and how you become one. Then each choose two of these verses and explain to the other what they mean: John 1:12, John 3:16, Romans 6:25, 1 Peter 2:24.

6. Finish by each praying for a friend you know who you think may be interested in discovering more of what it means to know God.

Moving forward

Aim

To encourage young people to reflect on what it means to trust God and to move forward to a deeper personal faith.

Preparation

This discussion activity is very simple and works best with a group of young people who are reasonably mature and have the ability to be quiet and to think. You will need Bibles, pen and paper, and copies of the Bible verses and questions.

Main session

1. Listed below are six Bible passages which express various aspects of what it means to trust in God as experienced by various biblical characters.

Give one reference to each member of your group, together with a list of questions.

Bible passages

(a) ABRAHAM: GENESIS 12:1–5
(b) MOSES: EXODUS 3:7–16
(c) SAMUEL: 1 SAMUEL 3:1–10
(d) ELIJAH: 1 KINGS 17:8–16
(e) MARY: LUKE 1:39–56
(f) PAUL: PHILIPPIANS 3:7–14

Questions:

(a) What does the passage teach us about trust in God?

(b) How can we best express by our actions what it means to trust God?
(c) What are the things which stop us personally from moving forward into a deeper trust and faith?

2. When each member of the group has a passage, ask them to find somewhere where they can be quiet and answer the questions. Emphasise that they should first be quiet and reflect on the passage so they can really feel something of what their Bible character was asked to do by God. You could tell them not to write anything for the first ten minutes but just to meditate on the passage. Give them plenty of time to reflect on the passage in the light of the questions. It might take anywhere from 10 to 40 minutes, depending partly on the maturity and spiritual sensitivity of your group.

3. When everyone has finished you can either have groups of people who looked at the same character, which would be particularly appropriate if you have a large group, or you can simply form one group and ask people to report back their answers.

Hints

It may be stating the obvious, but if the final group session is to be effective, you will need to have reflected on the passages and questions yourself.

The value of this style of session is that it allows individuals to understand and reflect but also gives opportunity for group teaching.

Emmanuel – God is with us

Aim

To strengthen individuals' awareness that God is always with them and will never desert them. When we acknowledge the power of Jesus in our lives and commit ourselves to following him, we begin to see things differently. We become more aware of God's presence in ourselves, in other people, in the world around us and in prayer and worship.

Preparation

The group or each group will need Bibles, pens and paper and also a prepared worksheet taken from the texts and questions below.

Main session

1. Divide into groups of five or six at most. Ask them first of all to share with each other just one incident in their lives when they have felt God was particularly close to them.

2. Then ask them to look at the passages below. You may wish to be selective and take only a few texts, or you may want to use all the passages. Get them to read each passage in turn and comment on each one. However, the comments should only be for around two minutes – it should not develop into a discussion.

   (a) Things went wrong – Genesis 3:8–13.
   (b) Moses' experience – Exodus 33:12–23, God promises to be with his people.

(c) Confidence in God's presence and protection – Psalm 16:7–11.
(d) God's complete knowledge and care – Psalm 139:1–18.
(e) God never forgets – Isaiah 49:14–16.
(f) God appears in person – Matthew 1:18–23.
(g) Right to the end – Matthew 28:16–20.
(h) Nothing can separate us – Romans 8:37–39.

3. Now ask them to discuss the following questions in the light of the passages:
(a) What do the passages tell us about God's presence?
(b) What do we discover about the plans of God and how he uses people?
(c) In what ways do you recognise God's presence in your daily life?
(d) In what ways do you think people see God's presence in you?

4. Finally ask each group to comment briefly on what they learnt from their discussion. Highlight the salient points in a brief summing-up. Finish by singing a suitable song or two that reinforces what you have been studying.

Bible character role play

Aim

To deepen individuals' understanding of what it meant for various biblical characters to trust and follow God.

Preparation

Choose various passages from the Bible which give the opportunity to explore the feelings of the characters. Here are three examples – but the list of possibilities is endless.

1. Luke 24:1–12: The women and the empty tomb.
2. Acts 9: 1–19: Paul's conversion and Ananias' vision.
3. Jonah 1: Jonah runs from God.

Main session

1. Work in one large group, or have a number of groups either dealing with the same passage or, preferably, with different passages on the theme of following God.

2. Choose the characters for the passage you have chosen. Ask someone to read out the passage, and then to read it again slowly. Then ask the characters to go away for 10–15 minutes to prepare for acting out the story.

3. Ask the group to perform the passage in front of the others. It does not have to follow the text exactly. Next get the rest of the group to ask the characters what they would feel if they really were the character concerned. Encourage them to ask questions which will bring out the emotional response of the

characters. Alternatively, if you do not want questions fired at the characters, ask them in turn to explain what they imagine their character must have felt. It will help if you are thoroughly familiar with the passage so that you can bring out the main teaching points.

4. Ask the other groups in turn to perform their role-plays.

SECTION VII

SOCIAL EVENTS

Introduction

The social side of your youth group is just as valuable as the more serious, overtly spiritual side. Do you know why? There are lots of reasons – here are a few.

Firstly, it is important that young people have fun together.

Secondly, the quality of the social relationships within the group will affect the church fellowship.

Thirdly, the young will often understand what it means to be a Christian and live as a disciple more from how you conduct yourself while taking them off on a social event than when you stand up and give the God slot. It's all obvious, isn't it! Or is it? I know some youth groups who have cut out a substantial part of their social programme so that they can concentrate on the teaching. This is a mistake on every account, and you will only produce distorted young people who will have a twisted view of the Gospel.

Here are ten suggestions for social events for your youth group. If you are a good youth leader you may already have done them, but if there are some you have not tried then give them a go.

One night stand

Preparation

Draw up a list of local centres where people work all night, for example, a police station, hospital casualty department, fire station, chemical plant or post office. You may also have local places of interest which are open twenty-four hours a day. Write to, or better still go and visit in person, each of the places you hope to visit, and get their permission. Then draw up an itinerary for the event. You will need to consider the logistics of how to get everyone from place to place. Walking is by far the best, but cars may be needed at certain points. You will need to obtain written parental consent for each of the young people, and make sure you have plenty of adult support – at least one adult for every seven young people. Finally, contact the local press because it is very likely that they would be interested in either a write-up or a photograph of the event.

Main activity

A suggested starting time would be around 10.00 p.m., finishing about 6.00 a.m. back at the group's meeting place for breakfast. This activity is best in the summer months when you have milder weather and more hours of daylight. Its value lies in the fellowship it creates through the shared experience and also the appreciation it fosters of other people's lives and work.

Multi-cultural evening

Preparation and activity

1. Choose a country or a culture for your theme. If your church supports a missionary, it would be good to choose that country.

2. Ask everyone to come dressed in the style of that country or, if you know they will not do that, get them to bring something that is associated with its culture.

3. Contact the relevant embassy and ask them to send you information or posters.

4. If you have chosen somewhere like China, get in touch with the local Chinese take-away and pick up an order so that you can share a Chinese meal together. Alternatively get the young people to bring along something themselves and share it all together. (This will obviously need co-ordinating otherwise you may end up with a hundred prawn-balls and nothing else.)

5. You can take the whole idea further and find someone who comes from that country or at least knows something about it, and can talk and show slides. They can also bring along local music. But take care that your speaker does not arrive armed with a thousand holiday slides and bore everyone. Kindly but firmly brief him or her so that the talk does not exceed around fifteen minutes. If you cannot get a speaker, try a short video.

6. If you can obtain some traditional music of that country, why not get everyone to have a go at a dance?

Beach barbecue

Preparation and activity

How far do you live from the sea? If it is less than two hours' travelling then this idea is a must for your summer programme. It is simple, slightly mad and great fun.

Hire a minibus or bus with a driver. Don't just use cars or the event will not be a notable success, because part of the fun is in travelling down to the coast together. The event begins when everyone arrives at your meeting place to go off together – not when you all arrive by various cars at the beach.

Take equipment for beach games and all the appropriate items for a barbecue – don't forget the firelighters! While the food is cooking you can swim or play games. If you bring a guitar and song books, you can have some informal singing at the end and on the way home.

It may seem crazy leaving at around six and going on a two-hour ride just for a barbecue. But I guarantee the idea will be a success because it's just a fun crazy thing to do. Also it is the sort of event where the teenagers can easily invite their friends along.

Hints

Know where you are going and make sure the beach is suitable for a barbecue and games. Remind everyone to bring warm clothing. Have an alternative activity up your sleeve if the weather is bad but only put it into operation if the weather is terrible. Approximate cost of the event could be as little as £2 each.

Tramps' supper

Preparation and activity

This social activity has a variety of names. I've called it a Tramps' Supper. It can be called a Progressive Meal or Running Supper. If you have not already done this event with your young people then it is a must. It can be great fun.

The idea is very simple. Choose three or four homes within walking distance of each other (say, ten minutes' walk) where each course of the supper can be eaten. In other words, one home for the starter, another for the main course, another for pudding and another for coffee. Then you need a little group in each home to organise the food. Keep the food straightforward and simple.

Make sure you know how many will attend a week in advance so you know both your budget and the numbers you are catering for.

Hints

Ask everyone to take off their shoes when they enter the house and don't forget to send the parents whose houses you are using a thank-you card after the event.

Try to keep the schedule running to time to avoid catering problems, for example, food not ready or, if you are late, burnt!

Variations

Do everything in reverse order, i.e. start with coffee and dessert. Or just have a dessert tramps' supper, with different desserts at each location.

Treasure hunt

Preparation and activity

This event needs to be carefully planned and organised. You can use cars, bikes or go on foot. But one note of caution – if you do use cars make sure everyone who drives has the necessary insurance cover for their vehicle.

You need someone to draw up a route and produce good clues. These need to be typed up and photocopied so that everyone has a copy. Remember to provide enough space to write in the answers. Don't make the clues too cryptic, otherwise it might prove to be too difficult; also make sure that the directions for the course are adequate. It is up to you how far and how long you want the event to be. Probably lasting around an hour to an hour and a half is appropriate.

Each team needs to be staggered in its start so make sure you have a stop-watch and keep a record of the time. The time and the number of right answers obviously are the two considerations to take into account when you announce the winner at the end of the evening.

A suitable prize for third, second and first place can act as a fitting climax to the evening. The event is best done in the summer when there is more daylight.

Lock-in

Activity

You can do this over a 12- or 24-hour period. I think that 12 hours is possibly better. What you do is simply this: you lock everyone in the church overnight. This is an unusual idea but can create a great sense of excitement and tremendous fellowship.

During the 12-hour period – you might choose 8 p.m. to 8 a.m. – you can have all kinds of input and a variety of sessions. For example, you can have a time when someone, or everyone, is involved in reading a book of the Bible. You can have prayer groups, meditations, talks, music, worship, drama, videos. If you get everyone to come along with some sort of contribution it can be a very powerful event. Finish off with communion and breakfast.

You can create a moving atmosphere in the church by using candles or subdued lighting. In many church buildings the architecture provides an interesting location. If you carefully plan the lock-in and aim to create a positive atmosphere it can produce a strong sense of fellowship and also a healthy identification with the church.

Hints

Obviously you will need to liaise with the relevant church leader. Don't forget to make sure the heating is put on if the central heating is on a timer. It is useful, if only for your own use, to have a rough outline of the programme of events over the 12-hour period. Serve tea and coffee at various stages.

Night hike

Preparation and activity

Don't ask me why, but this is always a popular event – I suppose because it is a crazy idea which no one in their right mind who appreciates sleep would do. But it can be very worth while and successful if it is well thought out and well prepared. You will need to consider the following points:

1. A letter to parents giving all the details of the event and obtaining their written permission.

2. details to all the young people involved with advice on clothing and what to bring, e.g. suitable footwear, waterproofs, etc.

3. a night with a full moon!

4. a pre-planned course that can be safely covered in three to four hours.

Book your own or another hall to camp in overnight which has facilities for cooking breakfast.

A suggested activity programme for the event could be:

9.00 p.m.	Arrival at hall
9.15–10.30 p.m.	Games
10.30 p.m.–2.00 a.m.	Walk
2.00 a.m.	Return and sleep
8.00 a.m.	Breakfast

Paper galore!

Preparation

This is a totally crazy idea, but the end result is visually stunning! Start about 2–3 months before by asking everyone to bring a lot of old newspapers along each week. Do not tell them what it is for. Find somewhere to stockpile the paper convenient to the room or hall where you meet. Buy a large number of rolls of sellotape (about one roll for every three people) and some Blu-tack.

Activity

When everyone has arrived explain that they have to cover the whole room or hall in newspaper – ceiling, walls, floor, windows, etc. Every inch of the room is to be covered. For the ceiling you may need some ladders, or you may want to suspend paper you have sellotaped together from one side to the other to create a false ceiling. Before everyone has finished send someone off to get some chips from the local shop, wrapped in newspaper, of course. When the whole room has been covered ask everyone to make some clothing to wear out of the remaining paper and then to put it on. And finally ask them to make an object of their choice out of paper. Then stop for chips. The visual impact of everything covered in paper is quite stunning, and very memorable.

Hints

Make sure you get permission first of all to do this activity! Bring along a number of cloths to wipe away the print marks when you take everything down. Make sure that no one uses sellotape on painted walls or ceilings, but rather the Blu-tack. It would be a good idea to supply plenty of soap for washing very dirty hands at the end.

Auction supper

Preparation

Set out the hall with tables and chairs scattered around in small groups. Provide some background music, and if possible some suitable decorations to create an atmosphere, e.g. posters or coloured lights.

You will need to find out about ten days beforehand how many are coming because of the catering arrangements. You will need first course, main course and dessert, and each person will bring one course with enough for three people. So when you have done your calculations ask the appropriate number to bring along the appropriate course.

Activity

Serve drinks as people arrive and put all the food on a table at the front. When everyone is present you can start the auction. Choose someone with a bit of flair for acting as your auctioneer to give the occasion a bit of sparkle and make it good fun. The auctioneer auctions each dish that has been brought along. When the auction is complete ask everyone to join up with two people who have got a course other than their own. They can now share together what they have purchased. (This is why each course needs to be for three people.) Serve coffee to finish.

The money you have collected from the auction can go to charity or some worthy cause – club funds?

Going places

Check this out

Every good youth leader should know of all the various activity centres locally. Work through this checklist to see if you have exhausted all the various social possibilities.

- dry-skiing
- boating
- ten-pin bowling
- ice-skating
- theatre
- cinema
- swimming/water shoots
- sailing
- windsurfing
- amusement park
- crazy golf
- water-skiing
- zoo

SECTION VIII

A TERM'S PROGRAMME

How to organise an effective and stimulating term's programme

Planning a programme is a bit like going on a journey. You need to know where you are, where you are going, what method you are going to use to get there, and where you will be stopping in between here and there. So here are some steps to guide you through a term's programme and then we'll put them into practice and draw up a programme.

Step 1: Where are you?
How old are your young people, what schools and colleges do they go to, how many have jobs, or are unemployed? What is the level of spiritual commitment? What issues do they face in living out a Christian life? Is the group friendly or unfriendly? Does it work as a group, or is it very individualistic?

Step 2: Where are you going?
Where does God want the group to go, what are God's targets for your group? This is where it is vital that the youth leader or leadership team spends time in prayer, seeking God's will for the youth group. The leadership needs to know both the long-term aim and the short-term aim of the youth group, i.e. 'Where do we want to be at the end of this term?'

Step 3: What method are you going to use to get there?
Will it be by teaching, by creating experiences, by Bible study, by one-to-one work, or by taking the group to Christian festivals? How fast do you want to get there? If you run will you leave some behind, and if you dawdle will others race on in front?

Step 4: What steps are you going to take en route?
What will the actual programme be in terms of session plans, putting together the nuts and bolts of a programme, resources, time, place, programme cards, etc.?

Step 5: Reviewing the journey
At the end of the term look back and ask: where did we depart from what was planned, what were the high and low spots, and where did people grow spiritually, or seem to fall away? A good idea is to produce a reaction card for the young people to make an assessment of the term's programme. This can be a planning resource for the next term's programme.

This is how a youth group in Surrey followed through the steps.

Step 1: Where are they?

Age:	14	4 boys	2 girls
	15	3 boys	7 girls
	16	1 boy	2 girls
	17	2 boys	

Schools, Colleges, Work:	10	–local comprehensive school
	2	–R.C. convent school
	4	–boys' public school
	1	–sixth form college
	1	–Girls' public school
	1	–apprentice
Spiritual commitment:	8	–committed Christians
	4	–confirmed but unsure of commitment
	7	–not committed/don't know what it's about
	2	–don't believe

Some of the most committed will pray out loud, read their Bible, etc.

Issues facing the group:	Sex
	Loneliness
	Alcohol
	Non-Christian parents
	Drugs

The group is not over welcoming to newcomers, but tries to be friendly to them, it tends to see itself as a collection of individuals rather than as a group.

Step 2: Where are we going?
The long term aim is to bring everyone to a faith in Christ appropriate to age and length of Christian commitment. In other words to see non-Christians converted and Christians grow in their faith. The aim for this term is to teach some of the Gospel basics, but also to address some of the other issues, e.g. the lack of group cohesion, etc. So that at the end of term the group is more welcoming and the members have a deeper understanding of the Christian Gospel.

Step 3: What method are we going to use to get there?
The boys in the group are very practical, so there must be a number of activities, whereas the older girls like discussion groups. No one likes the youth group being too school-like, so, up-front teaching is out. Bearing this in mind we want to see people challenged and responding to the Gospel.

Step 4: What steps are we going to take en route?

Christian basics:	1.	What is a Christian?
	2.	The life of Jesus
	3.	The death and resurrection
	4.	Pentecost

Issues facing the group	1.	Sex
	2.	Parents
	3.	Loneliness

Group issues	1.	Working together
	2.	Honesty and acceptance
	3.	Reaching others

For each of our headings we now need to create a session outline. Diagram (a) this gives the aim of a session, the resources available and the final form it will take.

Having outlined the resources, you can plan the session choosing what to include and what not to. It is helpful to write out a Session Plan as shown in Diagram (b).

Diagram (a):

Session Resources

Title .... Date: ....

Aim:...

Resources

People	Icebreakers	Programme outlines	Bible study material
e.g. leaders available, plus people who could be invited in.	games (as in Section II) to get people warmed up and set the mood.	Pre-planned programmes that could be adapted. (See faithbuilders, groupbuilders, peoplebuilders sections of this book.)	Bible study outlines on the topic.
Rooms	Games	Audio-visual	Bible passages
What space is available e.g. small rooms for Bible study, large for games, etc.	Activities that are fun but make a point, and in which winning or losing doesn't matter.	Tapes, videos, slide tapes, etc. Poster displays.	Any appropriate Bible passages on the topic.

Activity	Simulation	Art and craft	Role-play
Activities that would meet the session's aim.	Real life situations experienced in the form of a game.	Art and craft idea that would facilitate the session's aim.	Acting out in drama or word how people would behave in a situation.
Social event	**Other**	**Songs**	**Prayer**
Social event that could meet the session's aim.		Choruses, hymns or other music.	

Diagram (b):

Session Plan

Title: ....*Date:* ....

Aim

Warm-up:

Equipment:

Preparation:

Activity/main session:

Conclusion:

Hints:

At this stage you need the diary and your church calendar of events. Any special church events, e.g. mission, anniversaries, weekends away, can be included where appropriate. Similarly local joint church youth events or Christian concerts can be added into the programme. It is important that the young people see themselves as part of both the local church and the wider Church, so they don't feel isolated and that they are the only young people who are Christians.

Now decide the dates for each of the sessions and fit them into the programme. It might look like Diagram (c).

Diagram (c)

Meeting dates		*Titles*	*Session contents*
Jan	8	Loneliness	(Emotions on paper)
	15	The Life of Jesus	(Biblical Favourites)
	22	Working Together	(Radio St Stephens)
	23	ANNUAL CHURCH VS. YOUTH GROUP FOOTBALL MATCH	
	29	Death and Resurrection	(Jesus Files)
Feb	5	Parents	(My Family & Other Animals)
	12	Sex	(St Valentine's Day)
	19	JOINT YOUTH SKATING TRIP	
	26	What is a Christian? YOUTH SERVICE	(What Makes a Christian?)
	28		
March	4	Honesty/Acceptance	(I Am/You Are)
	11	PHIL & JOHN CONCERT	
	18	Pentecost	(Filled with the
	25	Social Event	Spirit)
	28	SPRING HARVEST	(Tramps' Supper)
April	1	No meeting as leaders and group are at Spring Harvest.	

You could produce a programme card like that shown below, to be handed out to the young people or posted to them before term starts. Photocopied double-sided A4 card produces cheap programme cards of either folded A5 or A6 size, that look good and help the young people to know what's happening in advance.

INSTEP meets on Fridays
from 8.00p.m. to 10.00 p.m.
in the church rooms,
everyone welcome.

Jan
8 Emotions
15 Biblical Favourites
22 Radio St Stephens
29 The Jesus File

Feb
5 My Family & Other Animals
12 St Valentine's Day
19 What Makes A Christian?
26 Skating Trip (3.00)

March
4 1 Am/You Are
11 Phil & John Concert (£1.50, 7.00 p.m. – minibus)
18 Be Filled with the Spirit
25 Tramps' Supper

For further details contact
Patrick Angier on Haslemere
56141.

SPRING
PROGRAMME

DATES FOR THE DIARY:

23 January
FOOTBALL: INSTEP vs. VICAR'S 11

28 February
YOUTH SERVICE: 10:30 a.m. St Stephens

29 March – 4 April
SPRING HARVEST (Minehead)

Don't forget Step 5 – reviewing the programe at the end of term!

All this may sound complicated, but it is worth the effort. It actually makes life lots easier, because no longer will you be stuck for what to do on a Friday evening. All you need to plan the programme is a heap of all your youth group resources, books, files etc., the leadership team, about three hours, and a liberal supply of tea and cakes.

SECTION IX
WEEKENDS AWAY

Ideas and suggestions for a weekend away

The title of this book is *Youthbuilders*. We chose this title because we want all the ideas and activities in this book to encourage and build up the young people that come along to your youth group.

No discussion of the build-up and strengthening process would be complete without mention of taking your group away for a week or a weekend. Why? Simply because so many powerful and useful things can happen. Look at just a few:

1. *Energy*: Taking a group away creates a sense of belonging and identity. It can create an immense amount of group momentum and energy which can do a lot to sustain and strengthen the group.

2. *Fellowship*: People get to know each other at a much deeper level when they go away together.
3. *Relationships*: Relationships between leaders and teenagers can be strengthened so you can have a greater pastoral care for the young people.
4. *Atmosphere*: You can create a powerful and caring identity over a weekend. The atmosphere can be more important than the activities you lay on.
5. *Teaching and Worship*: Because of the amount of time you have together you have a unique opportunity for teaching and worship.

Those of you who have been involved in taking young people away will need no convincing of its tremendous value. If you are just taking over a group – now is the time to start thinking and planning!

But before we go into the nuts and bolts of how to organise a successful weekend away let me explain in greater detail the advantages outlined above.

Energy

As I have said a weekend away can add a great deal of energy to a group and strengthen individuals' sense of belonging and identity within the club. Mind you, at the end of any good weekend you may feel totally exhausted, but of course I'm not talking about physical energy. Any group needs occasions to breathe fresh life back into itself. It needs to rekindle its sense of identity and its momentum. Where this is created the group will have the necessary energy and emotional power to keep it going week by week during its normal course of routine activities. The energy of a group will, of course, affect a whole range of things – the numbers that attend, its sense of enjoyment, its desire to do new things, and its concern to invite outsiders to share in the experience.

You will find that often you can achieve more in a week or

weekend away than you can in a whole term's programme. I cannot emphasise strongly enough how important and valuable a residential experience can be. So plug your group into this very powerful source of energy.

Fellowship

If a lot of your youth group go to the same school, then they will know each other pretty well; if they don't, which is often the case, then they probably only see each other in certain contexts. Put them together for a weekend however, and all sorts of valuable and fascinating opportunities develop.

The fellowship aspect of a weekend can start the moment everyone begins to arrive at your meeting place to go off for the weekend. There is an air of excitement and anticipation. Possibly a few nerves for those who have not been away before. But over the course of time they are going to share a lot together and they will inevitably get to know each other in a far deeper way. (I often come across people in their forties and fifties who used to attend the various camps run in our Diocese. They always mention what fun they had and what good friends they made, and often they are still keeping up the friendships that developed on those events.)

Some of the barriers that people put up at group meetings often disappear during the weekend. The images and posturing attempts melt away as people relate to each other in a deeper way over breakfast or chatting informally late at night – or in the early hours of the morning for that matter. Spot the red eyes at breakfast!

Sometimes there is a new level of honesty. Because people relax they are more open, they are less defensive about talking about their real concerns and doubts.

Relationships

It's late on Sunday night and the main part of the evening with the teenagers is over. You have half an hour, perhaps an hour, to chat to some of them, to get to know them a little better. But it's the end of the day, you are a little tired, work tomorrow, you want to get home to the wife/husband (delete as appropriate). You have to sell some tickets for the next event, put up some posters, make sure the coee and drinks are being served, stack the chairs away, shut all windows, put away the stereo and of course lock up and secure the building. You eventually get into your car when everyone has gone home and you remember that you meant to ask Katherine if her mother has come home from hospital, Trudy if she passed her exam, John if he was managing okay with his new Saturday job, etc. etc. Somehow the time just seemed to fly and you didn't manage to talk to half the people you wanted to.

Sounds familiar? Over a weekend you'll have plenty of opportunities to chat and exercise a genuine pastoral care for those in the group.

Think of it another way. How well do the young people know you? They see you at youth club, at church or on outings but these are pretty limited contexts. But on a weekend they see you first thing in the morning (a wonderful sight), over meals, during washing up, and cleaning up at the end. In fact they see you in all sorts of little situations which normally they would not relate to you in. If your family come with you on the weekend they will see how you relate to them, and this is potentially far more positive than all the talks or discussions on relationships, respect and so on.

Hopefully the event will also encourage a sense of respect for you as the teenagers see you at a deeper level. There should be a Christian integrity about the kind of person you are, your convictions and values as they see you handle people in circumstances that demand teamwork.

Of course respect is a two-way thing and it involves your respecting them as individuals. I find the best way to relate to teenagers is to treat them and respect them as adults. They will then usually behave in a mature and adult manner.

Atmosphere

One of the important aspects of my present job as Youth Ocer for the Diocese of Guildford is training youth leaders. We have all sorts of training events, but one very stimulating and important type of training is leadership weekends. One observation I have made is this: the atmosphere created on the weekend is crucial! Why? Simply because so much of what you are trying to achieve as a youth leader is expressed in the atmosphere you create. I hope that the youth leaders who attend go away from the weekends with ideas and information, but I also hope they go away with a sense of fun, warmth, energy, enthusiasm and enjoyment. I want them to understand that the type of atmosphere they have experienced is the type of atmosphere that they need to build towards in their youth group. The simple truth is that you could organise the most dynamic club programme in Western Europe, but if the young people who come along do not enjoy the atmosphere the whole thing would be a massive flop!

You can create a very powerful and positive atmosphere with the youth group over a weekend. Most of the work will be done for you by the teenagers and their natural human dynamic. However, it is important that you are aware at each moment of what the atmosphere is, how it can be directed, and how it can best be expressed through the icebreakers and activities that you choose to do. A skilful leader should be able to observe at any given moment what is the dominant atmosphere of the weekend and be able to act if it needs to be directed. For example, if one small group of girls look as if they are not part of what is going on, you need to act to draw them in. If one element of the group is being negative you need to know how to handle them, how to change the general attitude by perhaps talking to them or giving them some responsibility.

Teaching and worship

The amount of time available on a weekend gives you a unique opportunity to do some substantial teaching. You can have up to five or six sessions without running the risk of being too 'heavy'. You can really get stuck into a subject or theme which should allow the young people to explore what they know or think or believe on any aspect of the Christian faith.

A weekend can give the opportunity for some informal, lively and creative worship. It is often good to have as your climax a celebration of Holy Communion or breaking of bread. Remember, Communion is the one service that Jesus himself gave to us and he is uniquely present when his people come together to break bread in his name. It reminds us of all he has done for us and how each of us is precious in his sight.

Location

It may be a tradition in your group to use a particular location for your weekends away. However, it is worth keeping your eyes and ears open for other possibilities because you may discover other centres which have better facilities and are even cheaper.

You will need to start planning a residential experience about a year in advance – perhaps even earlier if you are planning to use a well-equipped popular centre. Consider the various possibilities:

1. *Christian residential centre*: A lot of denominations and Church organisations have their own youth residential centre. There are a great many available. They vary enormously from cheap hotels to ocean-going yachts. If you want details speak either to your church leader or your denominational youth officer. You might be pleasantly surprised at the wide range of centres available.
2. *County Council residential centre*: It is worth contacting the youth department at your local County Hall. Many County Councils run excellent residential youth centres that are both well equipped and cheap to hire.
3. *A church hall*: An obvious suggestion, I know, but strangely enough it sometimes never occurs to groups that you can use a church hall. There must be thousands of church halls all over the country, most of them under-used. The advantage is that they are often cheap to hire and of course you will have a local congregation on hand if you need any advice or information. Again speak to your church leader or youth officer.
4. *Youth hostel*: There are some extremely good youth hos-

tels all over Great Britain. If you are a member of the Youth Hostel Association (YHA) it is worth discovering where hostels are available. They are often in very good locations for outside activities. If you choose to take your group out of season you might find that you are the only people using the centre.

5. *A school*: If you run a large group or are considering a joint venture with other local youth groups, why not investigate the possibility of a school? There are a great many private schools in the country and sometimes they are keen to use their accommodation during the vacation periods. The range of facilities offered by boarding schools can be impressive. A lot of schools have a Church foundation so look sympathetically on Church groups.

6. *A camp*: In the summertime camping is of course a possibility, especially if you have the equipment and are prepared to put up with the British weather. Some centres already have the sites and tents in place, and you simply arrive with your group and your team of helpers. Another possibility is to use a farmer's field. That will, of course, require previous negotiation.

If you are intending to run a camping weekend it is important to organise the logistics carefully. For example, you will need to check the following aspects:

toilet facilities
acquiring tents
adequate cover in case of bad weather
a mess tent for cooking and eating
cooking equipment and storage of perishables
lighting
chairs and tables
electricity supply

If you need to borrow tents or a marquee, contact the local Scouts or Guides, who are usually happy to help and give advice.

General administration

After sorting out your location, there are a number of other important administrative details to deal with:

- letters to parents

- parental consent forms (for young people below the age of 18)
- consult with your clergy to make sure your weekend does not clash with a special church event
- booking forms
- publicity (parish magazine, posters, handbills, etc.)
- insurance for the weekend
- deposits
- organising the leaders and cooks
- transportation

Cost

Working out the cost of your weekend away is crucial. If you are attempting such a venture for the first time, it may be worth discussing with your vicar or church leader whether any loss can be underwritten by the church. The reason for this is that a camp or houseparty that is attempted for the first time is likely to produce costs which may not have been allowed for.

You may also have problems with the numbers who participate, which will affect the financing of the event. Calculating how many teenagers may attend a weekend can be a nightmare, particularly if there is no tradition of going away. If some key members of your group decide to attend the rest will come. If they do not, you know too well what the effect can be. But do not be despondent if you get a small turn-out. Those who do attend will go back and tell everybody what a great time they had, and next year you will find you have little trouble in persuading people to come.

If you are going to a residential centre you need to be very clear about what financial penalties are involved if numbers fall below your expectations, or indeed if you have to cancel.

What do you have to budget for with a weekend? The following should certainly figure in your reckoning:

- cost of the centre
- catering
- transportation
- outings

- speakers' expenses
- administrative expenses, postage and publicity

The weekend programme

You may wish to choose a theme for the weekend which relates to the spiritual programme. There are an infinite number of themes you may wish to develop; here are a few possibilities:

- an Old or New Testament book
- a particular aspect of Jesus' teaching
- a character or series of characters from the Bible
- a theological issue such as Love, Salvation, Peace, Power, Liberation, etc.
- issues of social concern and the Christian response

You may wish to invite a speaker who you know is gifted at communicatng with young people. A different face and a different voice may be helpful for the teenagers. It may also provide you with the time to concentrate on the general organisation and smooth running of the weekend.

There are, of course, any number of options for a weekend programme. Here are two suggestions which may give some ideas.

Programme 1

FRIDAY NIGHT

7.30	Arrival
8.00	Dinner
9.00	Introduction and icebreaker games
9.30	Worship and Session 1
10.30	Evening Drink (hot chocolate etc.)
11.00	Bed or late night video (depending on how strict you are and the age of your group)

SATURDAY

8.00	Wakey wakey i.e. Get up.
8.30	Breakfast
9.30	Session II
11.00	Coffee

11.30 Session III
1.00 Lunch
2.30 Outside activity – Swimming, ice-skating, ramble, ten-pin bowling, etc.
5.00 Tea
5.30 Indoor Games – table-tennis, snooker or organised games
7.00 Dinner
8.00 Session IV
9.00 Disco, concert or barbecue
11.00 Bed or Video

SUNDAY
8.00 Arise and shine
8.30 Breakfast
10.00 Plan Morning Worship (involving everyone in drama, dance, prayers, reading, music, communion etc.)
11.00 Coffee
11.30 Morning Worship (Session V)
1.00 Lunch
2.00 Closing Session VI
3.30 Clear up
4.00 Tea
4.30 Depart
6.30 Evening service in home church. (This can help the process of integration with the church and also inform the congregation of what the young people have been doing.)

Programme 2

FRIDAY NIGHT
8.00 Arrival and unpack
8.30 Supper
9.30 Introduction to the weekend

SATURDAY
8.00 Rise and shine
8.30 Breakfast

10.00 Morning session
11.00 Coffee
11.15 Video
12.00 Lunch
12.45 Swimming
3.30 Arrive back for tea
4.00 Walk
6.00 Dinner
7.30 Evening session
9.00 Video

SUNDAY
8.00 Wakey Wakey!
8.30 Breakfast
10.00 Planning service
11.00 Morning service
12.00 Walk
1.00 Lunch
2.30 Clearing up and going home.

Working with Teenagers

NICHOLAS AIKEN

Working with Teenagers is at once theoretical and practical, and sets new and bold targets for all those involved in youth work. There is a wealth of useful facts and advice to enable the youth leader to plan an interesting and varied programme.

Trade paperback 016493 160 pp

Crowdmakers

BOB MOFFETT

Bob Moffett uses his imaginative skills in suggesting ways of communicating the Christian Gospel to teenagers. An invaluable resource book full of practical ideas for all youth leaders.

Trade paperback 805880 160 pp

Prayers for Teenagers

compiled by NICK AIKEN

This is a book of real prayers. Prayers that take life seriously and that take God seriously too. These are prayers written by teenagers for teenagers, covering many different situations in life. All proceeds from the book go to the Prince's Trust for its work in supporting young people in Britain.